TOYOTA
FIFTY YEARS IN MOTION

Eiji Toyoda

TOY⊙TA
FIFTY
YEARS
IN

An autobiography by the chairman,
EIJI TOYODA

MOTION

KODANSHA INTERNATIONAL
Tokyo and New York

First published in Japanese in 1985 under the title of *Ke-tsudan: Watakushi no rirekisho* by Nihon Keizai Shin-bunsha.

Distributed in the United States by Kodansha Interna-tional/USA Ltd., through Harper & Row, Publishers, Inc., 10 East 53rd Street, New York, New York 10022. Published by Kodansha International Ltd., 2-2, Otowa 1-chome, Bunkyo-ku, Tokyo 112 and Kodansha Inter-national/USA Ltd., 10 East 53rd Street, New York, New York 10022.

LC 87-45215
ISBN 0-87011-823-4 (U.S.)
ISBN 4-7700-1323-x (Japan)
First edition, 1987

CONTENTS

Preface 7

Part 1: Growing up at the Mill 9

In the Beginning   11
The Oshikiri Mill   14
Uncle Sakichi   19
School Days   23
First Encounters with Cars   28
College Life   30

Part 2: Early Years at Toyota 37

Landing a Job   39
The Shibaura Laboratory   40
A Motley Crew   43
The Search for Parts   46
The Push for Domestic Production   48
In and Out of the Army   50
The Koromo Plant   53
Switching Over to Metric·   56
Roots of the *Kanban* System   57
Getting Married   59
Toyota–Nissan–Ford: The Venture That Wasn't Meant to Be   60
At War with the U.S.   62
The Toyota Group Reorganizes   65
Wartime Innovations   67
Last Days of the War   69

Part 3: Picking Up the Pieces   77

New Lines of Work   79
Death of the Vice President   80
A New Dealer Network is Born   99
At the Brink of Failure   100
Stateside   106
Special Procurements: A Helping Hand   112
A Last Tribute to Kiichiro and Risaburo   114

Part 4: The Road to the Top   117

Toyota Begins Making Cars   119
New Products, New Dealer Franchises   122
The Motomachi Plant   124
Toyota and Ford   128
The Auto Industry Regroups   130
Motorization Comes to Japan   134
President of Toyota   136
Auto Emission Controls: Finding the Answer   138
The Rotary Engine Talks   143
The Oil Shocks   145
The Toyota Foundation   148
The Toyota Technological Institute   150
The Toyota Central Research & Development Laboratories   154
The Institute for International Economic Studies   156
Toyota Merges with Toyota   158
The Doyen of Toyota Elders   162
Decisions that Count   164

Epilogue: The Road Ahead   166

Preface

I've never enjoyed dwelling on the past and once even made a private resolution to leave old memories alone. There's nothing to be gained from brooding over the past. I prefer instead to make a clean break and set my sights squarely on the road ahead.

This attitude was something I first learned from Hitoshi Shiio, who taught math and mechanics at the Eighth Higher School of General Education before the war. He was the son of the head priest at a temple in Nagoya that is the resting place for successive generations of the Tokugawa family of Owari, shogun rulers of Japan from 1603 to 1868. During class, he'd tell us time after time: "Do what you think is right and proper as and when feel you should, because that's what the heavens command of you. Go on, push forth in the way that you feel is right." In other words, he wanted us to act at once, without hesitation, whenever we believed what we were doing was good and correct. "That is the will of heaven," he would say. His words were an inducement to look to the future, not the past.

When I was awarded the First Class Order of the Sacred Treasure by the emperor in 1983, I realized all of a sudden that, after straining at the bit all my life, I, too, had reached the venerable age for such decorations. Receiving this award was like getting my grades after final exams.

Quite frankly, there aren't very many people around who have been working with cars for fifty years. Most of those I've been associated with all this time have already passed away. A lot will never be known to future generations unless I do the telling. That's how I became convinced that I should leave some kind of a personal account of myself and those I've known.

However, upon rereading what has been recorded here, I realize that there are a few points I've left uncovered that I feel deserve at least to be mentioned. Starting with the 1983 announcement of the GM joint venture, NUMMI, in Fremont, California, Toyota has continued with its move to internationalize operations. Examples include two new plants—in Kentucky, U.S.A., and Ontario, Canada—both scheduled to come on-line in 1988. Also, in June of this year a decision was made with Volkswagen of the Federal Republic of Germany to begin the joint production of Toyota's Hilux one-ton pickup at their commercial vehicle plant in Hannover. These represent just a few of the major commitments Toyota has made to date, and it still remains to be seen what kind of grades they'll receive. To be sure, though, the road ahead should prove as exciting as that of the past.

I would like to thank those at Nihon Keizai Shimbun, Inc., who helped in the preparation of *Ketsudan*, the Japanese version of my memoirs, and in particular Ko Morita, Tetsuo Ota, and Hisao Yoshimura for their advice and encouragement. I am most deeply indebted also to Masaaki Sato, deputy editor at *Nikkei Business*, for his invaluable assistance at every turn.

September 1987

Part 1

Growing Up
at the Mill

IN THE BEGINNING

By the time Toyota had gotten serious about automobiles fifty years ago, America already had one car for every four people. Believing that Japan, too, would see a day when there was at least one car on the road for every ten Japanese, Kiichiro Toyoda, the founder of Toyota, split off the automotive department from Toyoda Automatic Loom Works in 1937 and established it as a separate entity, the Toyota Motor Company.

In a country with a population of one hundred million, a car-to-people ratio of 1:10 adds up to ten million vehicles. Assuming a modest replacement rate of 10 percent a year, this gives an annual demand for new vehicles of at least one million units, which was certainly enough, we figured, to support an automotive industry. When we began producing cars in 1935, we felt certain that such a day would come sooner or later. A half-century has gone by since then. Today Japan has one vehicle for every three people, a higher ratio than the U.S. did as the world's largest auto-producing nation. But the road to the top was by no means smooth.

Just mention Toyota and anyone in Japan will immediately think of Sakichi Toyoda, the father of Kiichiro. In fact, one can't very well tell the story of Toyota without recounting the part Sakichi played in it all.

Sakichi, regarded as an eccentric all his life, was the oldest of three boys. My father Heikichi was next, and the youngest of the trio was Sasuke. They were like the legendary three Mori brothers of medieval Japan who were enjoined by their father, a sixteenth-century feudal baron, to stand together like three arrows that, when united, cannot be broken. The Toyoda brothers were the three arrows that built the foundation for today's Toyota Group.

My father helped Sakichi out in his business ventures. Sakichi had begun studying looms in his youth, but money for research was scarce. Scraping together loans from various sources, he started to build wooden spinning machines in 1894 and sold these to generate working capital. My father's job was to sell these in the Kanto area, which included Tokyo and Yokohama.

The first looms that Sakichi built were also made of wood, being really just improved versions of existing devices. Looms at that time were operated and powered by hand. Not content with this, Sakichi set out to build automated looms that ran entirely on outside power. Three years later, in 1897, he perfected the Toyoda power-driven wooden loom. Hearing of this, an enterprising local weaver by the name of Tohachi Ishikawa decided to give the new loom a try. He and Sakichi established the Otsukawa Cotton Cloth Company, which set up power-driven looms built by Sakichi and began to produce cotton cloth.

There was just one problem. The mill had been built, all right, but there was no power with which to run the looms. Without power the mill couldn't operate. So my father gave up selling spinning machines and tackled the problem of generating power. Motive power in those days was generally supplied by steam engines, so he bought a used steam engine and tried to run the looms with this. The looms didn't budge, however, because the steam kept leaking.

Faced with no other choice, they took the engine apart and found that the leaking was caused by worn piston rods. Although they knew that the problem could be remedied by turning the rods on a lathe, the mill was located in the middle of nowhere; there just weren't any lathes nearby. So they spent a whole night filing the rods down. When they put the steam engine back together again, it worked.

My father often told me hardship stories like this when I was small. A great deal of credit is unquestionably due those who strove to build power-driven machines in an age when power was still pretty much of a curiosity, but energetic individuals like my father who gave their all to make this a reality also deserve recognition. In this way, he and Sakichi set up a mill using steam-driven looms, and before long it had achieved something of a reputation.

That was just the start. Sakichi continued tirelessly to refine and improve his looms and in 1918 established Toyota Spinning & Weaving, a thousand-loom venture with an equal number of employees. Not long afterward, in 1926, he set up Toyoda Automatic Loom Works—the parent firm of the Toyota Group—to fabricate his looms efficiently and cost-effectively. Toyoda looms proved so successful in vitalizing the Japanese textile industry that Sakichi was approached by Platt Brothers, the world's top loom manufacturer at the time, with an offer to buy his patent rights. He agreed and in 1929 sold the rights for use of his patents outside Japan, the U.S., and China to the British firm for 100,000 pounds sterling. This sum he gave to his son Kiichiro as seed money to develop and test-build automobiles.

Sakichi was born in 1867; my father was born in 1875. That's a difference of eight years. Actually, although my father always said he was born in 1875, the family register lists his birth as 1876. He claimed that the register was off because notification of his birth wasn't made until a half-year later. In those days, when a first son was born, you invited in the neighbors and celebrated the occasion. Of course, someone from the town hall also came by, so it got recorded right away. But because children born later didn't matter as much, subsequent births often went unreported for quite a while. It seems that a half-year or so after my father's birth, someone inquired whether a baby hadn't been born there a while back, which finally prompted my grandparents to report his birth.

My father never told us his real birthday. All I know is that he was born in 1875, but I have no idea even now on what day or in what month he was born. He would always tell us his birthday according to the old Japanese not the Gregorian calendar. He'd announce suddenly: "Today's my birthday," and treat us all.

During the U.S. occupation after World War II, I remember being summoned to the General Headquarters (GHQ) of the

Supreme Commander for the Allied Forces, which was located near the Hibiya intersection in Tokyo. An official there asked me to give my father's name and birth date. When I hesitated, wondering which date to give, he looked at me with an annoyed expression on his face, as if to say: "Don't you even understand English?"

My father eventually parted ways with Sakichi and set up his own mill for weaving cloth, using, I imagine, Toyoda power-driven wooden looms. His mill served as a sort of testing ground for the looms that Sakichi built.

My mother, Nao, gave birth to me on September 12, 1913, after the mill had been built and operations there had begun to get well under way. By that time my father had become independent and, in a modest way, lord and master of his own castle.

THE OSHIKIRI MILL

The house where I was born was tucked into one corner of the mill site in a section of Nagoya City known locally as O-horibata—meaning "the moat's edge"—on the northern side of Nagoya Castle. Since the whole place was home to me, I was—in a sense—born at a mill. Although the castle was bombed and destroyed during the Pacific War, the house my father built stands even now.

I wasn't the firstborn. An older brother whom my parents had named Heihachiro—after Heihachiro Togo, a hero of the Russo-Japanese War—had died before I was born. This severe blow disheartened my father, and unable to bear children for the next two or three years, my parents were urged to adopt a son as future heir.

They had more or less reconciled themselves to doing so when I was born four years after my brother died at six. My parents, who had just about given up all hope of having more children, were overjoyed. This may explain why I was overprotected and frail as a small child. Having gone through my brother's death, my parents weren't about to take a second chance and grew alarmed at the first sign of illness in me.

We lived at Ohoribata until I was four. The house was located right next to a military parade ground and officer headquarters. I remember being carried piggyback to watch the military drills there. Right at the center of the grounds was a big cannon the artillery fired every day at noon. It served the same purpose as the noon whistle does today. I constantly pestered everyone to take me to see it fired, but was rarely taken along.

I don't remember how many people were at the mill back then, but I think we must have had about twenty women workers. My father moved the place to a new site in 1917 because the neighborhood had become built up with private homes, making further expansion impossible. This was during World War I. Business was probably good and so I imagine that the mill was making money and my father wanted to enlarge operations. The new location was just outside of a town called Oshikiri, so everyone referred to it as the Oshikiri Mill. At first the formal name was the Toyoda Textile Oshikiri Mill, but when it was incorporated it became the Toyoda Oshikiri Spinning & Weaving Company. This site was only about a mile from our house in Ohoribata.

The biggest events I can recall before beginning grade school was our move to Oshikiri and the birth of my brother Toshihiko soon after, in 1917. The main structure for the Oshikiri Mill had not been completed yet, so my parents and I were living in a room in the men's dormitory. Toshihiko was born on the far side of a dividing screen set up in the middle of the room.

My sister Momoko was born on March 10, 1920, and three days later my mother died. She probably had been unable to recover after the childbirth. All I can remember about my mother was her scolding me once for tumbling into a stream at my grandmother's funeral. She also got angry at me for the same reason one other time, when I fell into the river and got soaked on my way home from kindergarten; I had been riding a bicycle behind an older boy who had come from the mill to take me home. More than sixty years have gone by since she passed away, and today I don't even recall what she looked like.

However, I do have a vivid recollection of the funeral. It was customary at the time for the husband not to serve as chief mourner when a wife younger than he died. So, although I was only six, the role fell to me. My father didn't attend the funeral; he just paid his last respects at home. I can remember riding a rickshaw to the temple where the funeral was held, then going on to the crematorium.

Shortly after things had quieted down again following the funeral, I entered Enoki Elementary School in Nagoya City, just a few hundred yards from the mill. I went to the Enoki School for four years, then was transferred in the fifth grade to a new school affiliated with the Aichi Women's Normal School. That same spring vacation, I made a trip by myself to Osaka. I returned later to find that my grandfather had just died and went on directly to the funeral. This was my paternal grandfather, Ikichi, father of Heikichi and Uncle Sakichi. Even today, the house in Kosai, Shizuoka Prefecture, where my grandparents lived remains exactly as it was back then. It is now home to Toyota president Shoichiro Toyoda.

At first, the Oshikiri Mill made just woven cloth. But a spinning mill was later added and operations expanded, so that eventually the mill was making everything from yarn to cloth. The number of workers grew steadily, as did the size of the entire facility. In fact, the mill ultimately covered more than fifteen acres, about five times the size of the original site.

Electrical power still was not available when the mill was built, so steam engines were installed and the plant ran by burning coal. At night, those engines were used to run generators that supplied electricity for lighting. In other words, we generated our own power. Most houses back then, like my grandfather's in Kosai, had one light at most. Naturally, few homes near the factory had any lights at all.

I was itching to get my hands on those steam engines and try running them. I'd watch the factory hands at work every day, so I knew the procedures. I begged and pleaded with them to let me run the engines, but no one paid me any attention. This was during my first years at grade school.

The boilers were cleaned once a year. A worker would strip down to his loincloth, get inside the boiler while it was still warm, and scrape the walls free of deposits. I must have made a real pest of myself, but I managed to get inside on a few occasions myself. This gave me a good idea of what the interior of a boiler is like. Later, one of the courses I took in college was boiler design. I'll bet that of the seventy students in that class, I was the only one who had seen the inside of a real boiler.

Radio broadcasts began in Nagoya when I was in the fifth grade. I immediately set to work building my own receiver, vying with the electricians at the mill to see who could complete a crystal radio first. In those days, factory-built radios were so expensive that everybody built their own sets. You'd buy only those parts impossible to make, but everything else from the coil on down you put together yourself. There were no vacuum tubes. Instead, we used what you might call pretransistor devices. With these homemade assemblies, we managed to pick up transmissions fairly well, perhaps because the station was close by.

All broadcasts were live. The most popular programs in Nagoya back then were the Japanese minstrel ballads known as *naniwa-bushi*. It got to the point where Nagoya Broadcasting Station became known as the "minstrel station." The station also carried English courses, but the programs that probably got the most time on the air were the commodities quotations.

At the mill, we kept track of the quotations by phone. A spinning mill has to know how the market is doing every day. I, too, was forced to help out quite a bit. When a phone call came in, the person on the other end just rattled off a string of figures, so whoever answered had no choice but to write them down. Of course, at first I had no idea what all these meant, but when I persisted in asking the clerks to explain the figures to me, they'd grudgingly tell me a thing or two just to get me off their backs.

One day, my father threw me a problem to solve. "Suppose that the price of cotton on the New York market today is x cents," he said. "You take this cotton and use it to spin yarn from which you then make cloth to sell in China. Can you make a profit on it?"

This would probably be a tricky problem even today. To work it out, you had to know the dollar market. China back then was on a silver standard, so you also had to know something about the silver market, which was determined by the price in London for silver bullion. But the London market was quoted in pounds sterling, so you also had to keep track of the exchange rate between British pounds sterling and the American dollar. Finally, you had to reckon into the calculations the dollar–yen rate, all of which amounted to a tall order for a grade-school pupil.

Exposed as I had been to such talk of exchange rates from my grade-school days, much later (during the "Nixon shocks" of 1971), when the yen was floated against the U.S. dollar after remaining fixed at 360 yen for over twenty years, I gave a talk at Toyota on the subject. I explained that, although it had been possible to maintain the yen–dollar rate at 360 yen all those years because the dollar was so strong, a fixed exchange rate was wrong to begin with.

When I was a child, the mill served as a place of learning as well as a playground for me. I lived at Oshikiri until I graduated from high school at the age of nineteen. Later, under wartime regulations compelling a reorganization of the cotton spinning industry, Toyoda Oshikiri Spinning & Weaving merged with Toyoda Spinning & Weaving and three other companies to form the Chuo Spinning Company, which was eventually absorbed by the Toyota Motor Company. The forced merger left a number of plants idle, resulting in the sale of the Oshikiri Mill to Toshiba Corporation in 1943.

Until just recently, the house we lived in remained standing at Toshiba's Nagoya Plant, where it was used as an employee clubhouse. In the spring of 1984, I received a very polite letter from Toshiba asking for my permission to remove the building so they could make way for expansion of the plant. My father built the Hoko Inari Shrine at the mill, and even today Toshiba performs rites there to Inari, the popular deity of good fortune.

One thing I will never forget from my grade-school years is the Kanto Earthquake of 1923. The earthquake hit us on September 1 at 11:58 in the morning. I arrived home from school, where we had had an assembly to mark the first day of the new term, and was eating lunch with my family when everything started shaking. We quickly jumped outside, but little damage occurred in Nagoya. However, the Kanto area—as we soon learned—was a total shambles. Very little real news trickled in. A special edition of the newspaper came out, but didn't say much. So we went over to the newspaper office to get the story directly.

It so happened that Kiichiro, Sakichi's eldest son, was in Tokyo when the earthquake hit. With all traffic and communications cut, we had absolutely no idea whether he was dead or alive. Both Sakichi and my father were very concerned and decided to send someone to find out. But it was impossible to get to Tokyo because the trains weren't running. When Kiichiro returned three or four days later, the whole Toyoda family breathed a big sigh of relief.

Uncle Sakichi

Ikichi, my grandfather, was a carpenter. Carpenters were often without work, so they also farmed. I imagine that carpentry was how Ikichi made himself some cash income. Sakichi picked up the trade by watching his father. My grandfather probably taught him some of the rudiments, but parents are often not the best of teachers. So he apprenticed Sakichi to a master carpenter in nearby Toyohashi. Even the spinning machines Sakichi first built were essentially an extension of his carpentry work.

By the time I started going to school, Toyoda looms had become as famous as Mikimoto pearls and Suzuki violins. Sakichi was widely known, but perhaps because he was family to me, while he was still alive I thought of him only as Uncle Sakichi, never as "Sakichi Toyoda, King of Inventors."

He was very strict with his eldest son, Kiichiro, but gentle with me. Since Kiichiro was eighteen years my senior, I suppose Sakichi may have thought of me as more of a grandchild than a nephew. In any case, whether he saw me as nephew or grandchild, because he had no direct responsibility for me, he was free to act the part of the kindly uncle.

Two of my strongest recollections of Sakichi were our trip together to Shanghai and his love of kites. He built large kites by himself and flew them in May. Back then, I didn't understand why he flew his kites at that time of the year. Now I do. Fly a huge kite in the green, windy hills of May and it makes a great roaring sound. I can still picture him taking in the string while looking up at his kite.

Sakichi took me along with him on a trip to Shanghai during summer vacation when I was a second grader. In addition to Toyoda Spinning & Weaving, Sakichi built a plant called Toyoda Spinning & Weaving Works in Shanghai and spent a lot of time shuttling back and forth between there and Japan. When I accompanied him, the Shanghai plant had not yet come on line. Technicians and laborers were still installing equipment and running tests. I believe the plant Sakichi built there is still in use.

We stayed at a large Western-style house that Sakichi had bought. I learned something about exchange rates on that trip. In Shanghai, people used a ten-sen silver coin and one-sen copper coin that resembled the corresponding Japanese coins both in size and design. There also was a one-yen silver coin called a "dollar" that was about the same size as the U.S. silver dollar.

The day we arrived in Shanghai, Sakichi handed me about ten yen, saying: "Here, take this. You're probably going to need some pocket money."

Ten yen back then was a fair sum of money. Ten of those heavy coins felt as if they'd tear a hole in your pocket. On some days, a ten-sen coin would rise in value to eleven one-sen coins, and on others it would dip to nine one-sen coins. It amazed me the way the rate changed every day.

I remember asking my uncle about this once: "If you exchange silver ten-sen coins for the copper one-sen coins when the silver coins are worth eleven of the copper coins, then change the copper coins back to silver coins when the silver ones are worth just nine copper coins, you can make a profit, can't you?"

"That's right," he replied, complimenting me on my discovery.

I wondered how something like this could be, but neither Sakichi nor any other adult I asked was able to give me a clear answer. In the end, I decided that if a lot of people want one-sen coins, then these rise in price, but if people are clamoring for ten-sen coins, then the price of ten-sen coins goes up.

Akitsugu Nishikawa, who later became the plant director when Sakichi's health failed him and eventually served as an auditor at Toyota Motor, once gave me a pamphlet he had written on currency exchange, telling me: "Here's something I want you to read." The pamphlet began with the words: "Yesterday's yen is no longer a yen today, and tomorrow's yen will not be the same as today's."

Not so long ago, I heard by word of mouth that Uncle Sakichi's residence in which I stayed while in Shanghai more than sixty years ago was used until very recently to house a U.S. consulate. I was even shown photographs of the consulate, but these somehow didn't agree with my recollections. In March 1985, while on a trip to China, I went to have a look myself. As it turns out, I believe that the house which I recall was not the site of an

consulate, but rather a Japanese consulate. Of course,
certain of this, as my memory of those youthful days
that clear.

vve stayed in Shanghai for about two weeks. On the morning
of our departure for Japan, I remember sulking in bed because
I didn't want to return home. I don't recall what it was he said,
but without showing any trace of anger or irritation Sakichi
somehow persuaded me to come along and together we boarded
ship and returned home.

Later, he told my father: "Eiji must have been taken with the
cars over there. He just didn't want to come back." Prophetic
words indeed.

I caused Sakichi a bit of trouble shortly before his death. A family
meeting was held to discuss my going on to high school. Sakichi
was ill in bed, so my aunt Asako (Sakichi's wife), my father, and
I all gathered at Sakichi's bedside to reach a decision. I strongly
suspect that he was no longer fully conscious then.

Sakichi was opposed to me continuing my studies. As my aunt
put it: "Going to school will be the end of you. A child as frail
and sickly as you will die, and that would be a big loss to the
Toyoda family."

My father wouldn't come right out and say it in front of his
elder brother, but he wanted me to go to high school. When
Kiichiro was admitted to Tokyo Imperial University, Sakichi had
been against his son going away to school, but my father convinced Sakichi to let him go. Soon after starting classes, Kiichiro
fell ill and had to take a year's leave of absence to convalesce.
In Sakichi's eyes, college must have been a place where one got
sick. When it came to my turn, my father thought it best to get
his elder brother's okay before sending me off to school, "lest
he complain later that we didn't consult him on the matter."

The conclusion reached at our little family conclave was that,
having been accepted by the school, I should at least be allowed

to take a crack at it. Sakichi died on October 30, 1930, the year I entered high school.

Seven years later, in 1937, a grade-school textbook came out giving the biography of "Sakichi Toyoda: King of Inventors." By that time I had already graduated from college and entered Toyoda Automatic Loom Works. The year before, when Kiichiro and I proofread the textbook, I was made aware once again of Sakichi's greatness.

SCHOOL DAYS

I entered the First Middle School of Aichi in 1926. The emperor Yoshihito passed away in December of that year and Crown Prince Hirohito ascended to the throne. The following year, the army staged major maneuvers on the outskirts of Nagoya. We students, too, were made to shoulder guns and march for inspection before the new emperor.

At the time that I entered Aichi Middle School, it and Meirin Middle School were the two most prestigious schools in Aichi Prefecture. Meirin had a distinguished history, having been established by the lords of Owari Province in the Tokugawa period (1603–1867). Aichi Middle School, on the other hand, had been preceded by the Aichi English School, which was established during the Meiji period as a national high school. The most illustrious graduate of our school was Shoyo Tsubouchi, the foremost Shakespearean scholar and translator in Japan and a well-known writer and critic.

At middle school, I entered the kendo (Japanese stave fencing) club. Everyone had to join one sports club or another. I chose kendo for no reason in particular, except that somehow it looked like a good choice.

All general school events were conducted with the students divided up into their respective sports clubs. During an athletic meet, the teachers had everyone assemble and took roll call. After that, they'd just wander about the playing field checking on each of the events. If you wanted to, you could slip away undetected. Still, because the students were organized into and supervised by sports clubs, if you did decide to play hooky, you were always found out. Once discovered, you didn't get off lightly, either.

Athletic meets also were somewhat unusual. Each club hosted its own sport. Thus, in the case of the kendo club, for example, contestants from other clubs, such as the baseball, sumo, judo, and tennis clubs, competed in a kendo tournament with members of our club acting as the referees. This was done with all the sports for which we had clubs, but no parents ever came to watch our meets.

The school had four classes at each grade level. The makeup of the classes changed each academic year, based on the grades of the students, so quite a few students in the same graduating class never had a class in common. The sports clubs were entirely different. There, you got to know all the members very well, including both upper and lower classmen. Personal contacts and friendships were much stronger between members of the same club than between classmates.

The kendo club always held practice during summer and winter vacations. Graduates of the school who had been in the club and were now in high school or college would come back and teach us, training us hard. I enjoyed the sport, but was not particularly good at it.

Every year at the school, the students would hold a strike for one or two days. I think it was sort of a movement against some of the teachers. Fifth-year students formed the nucleus of the strike, while underclassmen got a vacation out of it. Being a stronghold of staunch traditionalists, the kendo club always opposed the strike and continued to hold practices at school while it was in progress.

Someone always took the rap when a strike occurred. Strike leaders were suspended or expelled, and things became very uncomfortable for any targeted teachers. Given that the whole affair was only something concocted by middle-schoolers, such harsh punishment hardly seemed justified. In any case, this was one annual event that always left an unpleasant aftertaste. Fortunately, I skipped out of my fifth year and entered high school directly, so I never did take part in the strike, although classmates of mine who remained behind did.

While in middle school, I went all the way to Tokyo once to see the Graf Zeppelin, which had come over from Germany. The dirigible had flown nonstop all the way to Japan via Siberia. It touched down at the military air base at Kasumigaura, a short way from Tokyo. After being serviced in a hangar at the base, if flew off across the Pacific on its way to America.

My father gave me permission to go and see it, so I took a night train from Nagoya and arrived at the base the next day. The dirigible completely filled the inside of a large hangar, dwarfing a Japanese airship tucked along beside it. That's how big it was. After taking a good look at the zeppelin, I returned home again by night train.

The daily pattern was pretty well set during my middle school days. In the morning, I'd go to school and attend classes. Once these were over, I went to kendo workouts until about five o'clock, then returned home. We'd eat supper at about six, after which I took a bath and went right to sleep. Considering that I didn't study very hard, my grades were fairly decent.

The year I graduated, less than a hundred students continued on to the Eighth Higher School of General Education. This number included fifth-year students, fourth-year students, as well as middle school graduates who had failed the high school entrance exams in earlier years and were gunning for another chance. Of this total, about twenty were fourth-year students, myself included.

The freshman class at the Eighth Higher School was divided into seven groups, four devoted to studies in the sciences and three to the humanities. There were about forty students to a group, and I think the school accommodated around two hundred students per grade. We also had some repeaters, however, so there may very well have been more than two hundred altogether.

The students were divided into A and B sections for both the humanities and sciences. Students in the A section were required to take English as their first foreign language and German as their second. For students in the B section, it was the other way around: German was the first language and English the second.

My intention from the start was to enter the science–A section curriculum. I had taken the entrance exam in my fourth year of middle school fully expecting to fail it and was therefore not overly concerned about how I did. As it turned out, however, I passed.

Once in high school, I did pay attention to my studies, but also managed to enjoy myself without working too hard. Some of the students really hit the books, while others did nothing at all. I'd say I was about midway between the two extremes.

Mah-jongg started growing popular at about the time I entered high school. I had already been playing the Shanghai version of the game since middle school. Someone at the spinning and weaving mill Uncle Sakichi had built in Shanghai had brought my father a mah-jongg set as a present. He taught us the rules, and the game spread like wildfire at the Oshikiri Mill. One has to have four players for a game of mah-jongg, but with all the office and mill workers around, there was never any shortage of participants. However, by the time I entered high school, when the game began to catch on everywhere, I had had my fill of it and stopped playing altogether. I guess you could say that I graduated from mah-jongg in middle school.

I was asked to join the kendo club, probably because I had been a member at the middle school, but instead I chose gymnastics. I'm a little overweight now, but when I entered high school, if anything I was on the thin side: I weighed only about 110 pounds. I began working out on the high bar in middle school, and because the guys I was doing it with entered high school with me, we worked out together there too. Officially, we were neither a club nor a team—more like a group of friends sharing a hobby together. After we graduated, this group eventually took on the status of a full-fledged club, so our efforts bore some fruit. Gymnastics lately has become a showy affair, sort of like acrobatics, but it wasn't that way at all when we were at it. The reason I like the sport is because there's no need for a partner. It's something you can do alone.

During the spring and summer breaks, I usually went on trips. Starting back in grade school, I'd made several trips to Osaka and Tokyo, where I stayed at the homes of business associates of my father's and saw the local sights. We had relatives in Utsunomiya, just north of Tokyo, who took me to see places such as Nikko and Shiobara, a hot spring resort. In Nikko, they've now got a paved road snaking up the long slope called Irohazaka, but when I visited the place as a boy, we walked all the way up to Lake Chuzenji. It was March and there was still snow left on the ground.

I started mountain climbing and skiing in high school. While I had hiked in the foothills during middle school, I only began climbing the bigger peaks in high school. The first outing I recall was to Hakuba in the northern Japan Alps.

The first time I took to the ski slopes was at the foot of Mt. Myoko, a volcano in Niigata Prefecture. When I was still new to the sport, I had a hard time containing my impatience for it to snow. The closest spot to Nagoya was Mt. Ibuki, which was visible from the house. Back then, there were no daily updates on skiing conditions such as we have today in the newspapers and on TV. Instead, I looked out my window at Mt. Ibuki and tried to gauge the slope conditions.

Part of my summer vacations in high school was always set aside for practical training at the spinning and weaving mill. I had also gone through the motions of training in middle school, although this was not at our plant but at the Aoki Dye Works, a dyer in Tokyo that my father did business with. I spent two weeks there, helping out in any little way that I could, although

I didn't do much of what you'd call real work. At the dye works I received an allowance more than adequate for what I was doing, but my father never paid me any wages when I underwent training at our own plant.

It wasn't until much later that I found out that I had been a "managing director" of Toyoda Oshikiri Spinning & Weaving while in middle school. Not only that, when he enlarged the plant, my father took out some big loans for which I was jointly liable— as a middle school student! That's one of the seamy sides of privately run businesses. Yet, because I was only nominally a part of management, I didn't draw a salary.

When I traveled to India on company business in 1984, in addition to the auto plants I had gone to see, I also toured some spinning mills where I saw the same machines that I had trained on and sweated over during high school at my father's plant. Talk about nostalgia!

First Encounters with Cars

I got a chance to see many different cars on my trip to Shanghai with Uncle Sakichi during the second grade, but although I was definitely interested in them, cars were not familiar and accessible to me then. Soon after that trip, my father spent a half-year traveling abroad. When he returned, he brought back with him a German electric car.

He went to register the car with the police and get some license plates, but there were no plates for electric cars. The police didn't quite know what to do, so they gave him motorbike plates. That meant that only someone with a motorbike license could drive the car. This being an electric car, we'd charge the batteries overnight, but it still wouldn't run very far. Even today, this remains the biggest obstacle to the widespread use of electric cars.

The car had a steering bar instead of a steering wheel. There was a forward and a reverse gear, but only two speeds, high and low. In low, the car crept at a snail's pace, but switch it into high and suddenly you'd be barreling along at full speed. That was the only speed control there was. In high, you'd go over the speed limit, but since cars were still a rarity back then, the police were lenient. People took things easier in those days.

Cars for me were something fun to watch and ride, but as I was only in grade school, it never occurred to me to want to drive them. Naturally, I hadn't the slightest idea that someday I would become intimately involved in the automotive industry.

The popularity of the car began to spread rapidly in the late 1920s. While I was still in middle school, the newspapers would carry ads for cars just about every day. Just like children today, back then many kids were fascinated with cars. Some of my classmates even cut out the ads and collected them. Of course, virtually all the motor vehicles sold in Japan were American or European makes, since Japan was producing very few cars to speak of. The sudden advent of the automobile in Japanese life was the result of fierce competition between U.S. and European automakers for the control of what they viewed as a promising overseas market.

The number of buses rose rapidly at about the time I was starting high school. Nagoya had a streetcar service run by the city, but small bus companies began popping up one after another. Several of these companies were located in front of the main railway station, where conductors would hail passersby to draw in customers. Instead of calling these outfits by their proper names, everyone referred to them as the "blue bus," the "red bus," the "silver bus," and so on, in allusion to the color of the bus body. Because of that, Nagoya became famous for its "buses of seven colors."

The sudden rise in the use of buses to get around led to a crunch in the city's streetcar service. Deciding that it would be wiser to expand bus services rather than the streetcar system, the city started up a municipal bus service. The private bus companies used "bus girls" as conductors, but the city for some reason used male conductors.

Sometime later, when I was going to college in Tokyo, there

were a lot of "yen taxis." At first, the drivers charged a yen, but competition drove the price down so that you could get a ride in style for all of fifty sen, which was equal to a half-yen. But, being the penny-pinchers that they were, college students would do their best to beat down the price even further. Yen taxis didn't have meters, so the passenger and driver would haggle over the fare. Once they agreed on a price, the passenger would get in and be on his way. When there was a college baseball game at the stadium near the Meiji Shrine, we'd take a taxi over from Hongo, where the university was located. One of us would hail the taxi and negotiate with the driver. Thinking that he was getting just one rider, the driver would agree to a low fare. Then we'd come out of hiding and pile into the car. We did it partly for kicks, but managed to get to the stadium this way for just five or six sen apiece.

These years were the heyday of the car in the period before the war. Once the war got under way, however, what with fuel rationing and other controls, passenger cars rapidly faded from the scene.

COLLEGE LIFE

In 1933, I entered the faculty of engineering at Tokyo Imperial University, where I majored in mechanical engineering. During my first year at school there, I stayed at a boardinghouse in Hongo. The place was very conveniently located, just in front of the main gate in fact, so it took me less time to get to the campus gate than to go from there to my classes.

In my second and third years, I moved to a dormitory for students from Aichi Prefecture, located some way off in Koishikawa. I walked to and from campus every day, rarely taking the streetcar. It was a straight walk in, so I could get to school much faster this way than by streetcar, which made a big, roundabout loop. Since I stayed in Hongo for another year after graduating, I spent a total of four years in Tokyo.

While a student at Todai, which is what we called the university, I had plenty of time on my hands, which enabled me to visit the various local sights. During breaks between terms, I returned to Oshikiri. No one stayed around at the boardinghouse and dormitory, so there really was no point in remaining behind.

I spent part of my summer vacations during my freshman and sophomore years getting some hands-on experience at Toyoda Automatic Loom Works, but I also found the time to travel a bit with my friends at college. During my first year at school I went to Hokkaido and in my second year I traveled to Kyushu. A number of sites around the country were being designated national parks under the National Parks Act of 1931, so we traveled around visiting these. I figured that I'd have plenty of opportunities in the future to see the big cities, such as Sapporo, so I sought out places that were relatively unfrequented, like Akan National Park in Hokkaido.

Akan National Park is located in eastern Hokkaido. When I went there in 1933, there was already an automobile road linking Teshikaga with Akan. Curious as to why this should be in an age when cars were still something of a rarity even in the larger cities, I asked the conductor on our train about it. He replied: "There are bears on that road. The only safe way to travel is by car."

Electric lights had hardly made an appearance yet around Lake Akan; everyone still used kerosene lamps. The inn we stayed at was different, however. It had just recently been built and so was equipped with modern conveniences, including electric lights. Unfortunately, the generator broke down the day we arrived. The manager asked us to take a look at the problem, but although we were engineering students, we were still in our first year, on top of which everything was so dark that fixing anything on the spur of the moment would have been an impossibility.

We had another surprise in store for us that same day. The rooms were pitch-black, so we went for a walk by the lake. When we came back, the people at the inn asked us whether we hadn't run into any bears.

On my trip to Kyushu in southern Japan, I again made it a point to visit places I would be unable to see after graduation. I hiked up Mt. Aso along a back route, then climbed down the front of the volcano. As I was boarding a bus for the return trip, the conductor asked me: "Where's your ticket?" Now I had walked up the mountain and back down, so of course I had no ticket. But the conductor refused to be swayed by my explanations. "You've got to have a round-trip ticket to ride this bus," he declared smugly.

Back then, people often committed suicide by flinging themselves into volcanic craters, and one even had to have a round-trip ticket to ride the ferry from Tokyo to the nearby island of Oshima. That may be where the bus service at Mt. Aso picked up the idea.

Anyway, I did my share of traveling and mountain climbing.

On-site factory training during the summer vacation was a course requirement during my third and final year at college. I was sent to undergo training at the Kawasaki Car Manufacturing Co. in Kobe, which was making steam locomotives and buses. I got off work at five o'clock, then went swimming with the other workers at the beaches close by. The training period lasted for a full month, but my stepmother, Teru, died while I was there, so I had to take a week off to attend the funeral.

I particularly enjoyed the festival that the engineering faculty put on once a year at the Koishikawa Botanical Garden. We'd have draft beer brought in by truck. Students supplied the buckets and dippers. More beer was downed on that occasion than at any other time of the year. I wasn't very much of a boozer myself but I got a big kick out of joining in all the fracas.

One honor of which I'm proud was my being awarded the West Prize upon graduation. This was named after Charles Dickinson West, an Irishman who had taught engineering at Tokyo University early in the Meiji period (1868–1912). West had died in Japan and his inheritance was used to set up a trust from which funds were dispensed as prizes to mechanical engineering students of high academic standing. The year I graduated, I believe there were seven or eight recipients, including myself and Ryoichi Nakagawa, who is a former director of Nissan Motors. During graduation, we went together to West's statue on campus as a gesture of thanks, then paid our respects at his grave in Aoyama Cemetery.

Sakichi's wife, my aunt Asako, passed away one cold day in January 1936. I received news of her death while attending an automobile show and returned to Nagoya at once. During her last years, my aunt had stayed at home working on a bust of Sakichi. Today the bust remains at Sakichi's birthplace in Kosai.

The February 26th Incident, which played an important part in the events leading up to the Sino-Japanese War of 1937–45, occurred not long after I returned from the funeral. I was working hard on an engine design as my graduation thesis and would go onto campus whenever I pleased and spend long hours at the drafting board. The day the incident occurred, hardly anyone had showed up by noon. I began to wonder whether the snow had made traveling difficult, when people started showing up and I got word that a coup attempt had taken place.

News came trickling in slowly. We learned afterward that a group of junior army officers backed by a large contingent of troops had risen in rebellion, seized control of parts of the city, and assassinated several key government leaders in an attempt to force political reforms. Before we knew it, the campus was buzzing with unfounded rumors that Todai would be attacked by the army as a seat of leftist sentiment. Some of my classmates began worrying that if the confusion persisted, they might not be able to graduate, while others brightened at the prospect of possibly being able to graduate without having to complete their final drawings. The professors, concerned over our safety, sent us home, telling us that remaining on campus might be dangerous.

The next day, I walked over to where the incident had occurred. There was no other way of getting there, as all transportation had come to a standstill. I walked in front of the Diet Building. The rebel forces had occupied the National Diet and hung large banners from the windows.

Next, I went by the prime minister's residence. The road near the residence was barricaded and machine guns were in position. Had I gone any closer, I probably would have been bayoneted. Since I wasn't about to get injured for no reason at all, I beat a hasty retreat. Prime Minister Okada was at that very moment hiding from the rebels in a closet within the residence.

After that, I went over to the navy ministry. Dusk was falling when I passed along the side of the ministry, but I could see something glinting above as I walked outside the compound walls. When I took a closer look, I realized that there was a row of bayonets running along the top of the wall over my head. Later I found out that the navy had assembled a fleet of warships in Tokyo Bay and was prepared to shell the rebels' positions. I get a cold sweat every time I think about how I walked along that wall jam-packed with soldiers ready to shoot.

Over the next couple of days I wandered about these and other spots where the incident had taken place. On the third day I went over to the martial law headquarters. Machine guns were in place there too. The military forces out to crush the rebellion wore white headbands.

The famous appeal by the army to the insurgent troops, "Now is not too late," calling upon them to defy their leaders and assuring them that they would be pardoned if they returned to their barracks at once, was issued on the fourth day, I believe. If the insurgents failed to respond to this appeal, then the army would be forced to distinguish between its supporters and the rebels, so a general curfew was imposed at this point. I returned to my dormitory in Koishikawa and stayed put, listening to developments over the radio.

The rebellion was quickly suppressed and things returned to normal again within about a week's time. As it turned out, my classmates and I were not exempted from the requirement to submit a final design. The design I prepared was for an automobile diesel engine. After submitting the drawings, we had to undergo an oral examination on our designs. Like defendants in a trial, we were called in one by one. Once we had cleared this final hurdle, we were graduates at last and out on our own.

Part 2

Early Years at Toyota

LANDING A JOB

One day before summer vacation in my senior year at Todai, my faculty advisor called me in and asked me: "Are you planning to work for the government?"

As I recall, quite a few Todai graduates were entering government service at the time. Even among the engineering students, five or six joined the Railway Bureau, while a few others went over to the army and navy ministries. I immediately answered that I detested the idea of becoming a civil servant.

"Well, then, I've got an offer here from a good private company. How about it?"

Although I had no intention of going into government employ, I had not yet decided where I wanted to work. I told my adviser that I would go home for the summer break and think the matter over carefully.

When I returned home for the summer, I talked this over with Sakichi's eldest son, Kiichiro, the founder of Toyota. I was seriously considering my adviser's offer, as I felt that I could always make a living elsewhere for a while before coming back to work for Toyota. The company was nowhere as famous as it is today, so I believed that it would take me in whenever I wished to return.

But Kiichiro thought otherwise. "Look," he said. "Now that you've started working with cars, don't throw that away by going to work for someone else. Come and join us."

My father also had me in mind to take over someday at the Oshikiri Mill. But Kiichiro was adamant: "Eiji's coming with me." And that was that. With me now out of the picture, my father started preparing my younger brother Toshihiko as his eventual successor. That's why he sent Toshihiko to a textile school. When my brother was killed in Guam during the war, this sent my father into another deep depression.

At school, we were supposed to submit a form indicating our job preferences after the summer break. I drew a line through the "Employment" section and filed the papers. The college double-checked with me, asking if there really wasn't anything they should do for me. I simply answered "No" and went on home. That one word is how I got started in the automotive industry.

Kiichiro and I were first cousins. He had just started building cars and still had very few able assistants, which is probably why he pinned such high hopes on me. There was a tacit understanding between us on this. One day, when I told him, with a touch of rancor, that I had handed in my job preference form at Todai with "Employment" crossed out, he responded: "I wrote 'self-employed' on mine."

Toyoda Automatic Loom Works made the decision to begin developing and producing motor vehicles in a board meeting held in December 1933, the year I started college. Since I was majoring in mechanical engineering, I returned to the company for training during the summer and winter vacations. An automotive department had been set up in which engineers were test-producing tiny engines that they mounted on bicycles. I myself wasn't involved in building the engines, but I did spend a lot of time riding around on the motorized bikes. So my association with cars actually began before I graduated from school.

THE SHIBAURA LABORATORY

After graduating from Todai, I entered Toyoda Automatic Loom Works. Kiichiro's first orders were to set up a research lab at Shibaura in Tokyo. For some reason—perhaps he wasn't getting along very well with Risaburo Toyoda, husband of his sister Aiko and the first president of Toyota Motor Company—Kiichiro had decided to live in Tokyo. He found a house in Hongo and I went to stay there too. I didn't pay any rent, so in a sense I was sponging off him.

Kiichiro's family also moved into the house, and his oldest son, Shoichiro, now president of Toyota, went to grade school nearby at Seishi Elementary School. Shoichiro sat for entrance exams at two or three middle schools the following spring. Kiichiro was incredibly busy and all Shoichiro's mother, Hatako, could do was worry, so I accompanied him to the exam centers. He eventually got into the First Middle School of Tokyo and I attended the commencement ceremony in place of his parents.

Kiichiro had told me: "Go set up a lab at the car hotel in Shibaura." I was to do this entirely by myself.

"Car hotels" back then were something like the large commercial garages we have today. Regulations for garages were a lot stricter than they are now. To own a car you had to have a place to park it. A car held gasoline, so a vacant lot wouldn't do. Cars had to be kept in fire-resistant structures. I don't know whose idea it was, but to accommodate car owners Toyota had jointly set up with a number of other concerns a company called the Car Hotel. This was a three-story ferroconcrete affair with a fireproof, flame-resistant construction. In those days, only the well-off had cars in Japan. Usually these were driven by full-time chauffeurs who would take the masters home in the evening, then return the cars to the garage. The next morning, the chauffeurs would pick up their bosses at home and take them to work.

The drivers lived in an apartment building adjoining the garage. My job was to set up a lab in one corner of the building. It was the kind of place where, in autumn, when the chauffeurs' wives were broiling fish, the odors would come drifting into the room.

The first thing I did was clean the place up. Then I bought some desks and chairs, drafting boards, and rulers so that I could at least do some drafting there. For the longest time nobody came to join me, but a year later, when I prepared to return to company headquarters in Kariya, we had close to ten people working there.

Even for a research lab, it was a very casual and relaxed place. In the beginning, I was even commuting there in my student uniform. Not that I particularly liked student dress; it's just that I didn't have a regular jacket yet.

After setting up the lab, my first project was to do some research on machine tools for manufacturing cars. We called it research, but I didn't know the first thing about machine tools, so it was plain book studying more than anything else. For my efforts I received a daily allowance of 1.7 yen plus another half-yen for meals, or a total of 2.2 yen. I got paid once a month.

The Car Hotel also had a car service center. This provided service not only to cars kept at the hotel but to all Toyota products in the Tokyo area. Every time a car was sent back for one problem or other, we knew about it. Actually, checking these defective cars over was one of our jobs, although this was not directly related to our work at the lab.

One day, Kiichiro bought a small French plane called a Pou, meaning "louse" in French. This was just a one-seater and so was of little practical use. What we did instead was take the engine apart. I made a sketch of everything, but that's all we ever did with it. We never even tried to build it.

Predictably enough, Kiichiro next had us studying the helicopter. This was before the first practical helicopters had been made. I knew that planes with rotating airfoils were called autogiros, but had no idea how these were built. Learning that the army air unit at Tachikawa had one, I went over to take a look. It lay off in a far corner of a warehouse on the base. An autogiro has a propeller at the front, like a regular airplane. When it taxies, the airflow causes the airfoils on top to rotate and supply lift for takeoff. But the army's autogiro apparently didn't work the way it was supposed to.

At Shibaura, all we did with helicopters was study them, but when I returned to company headquarters in Kariya, we test-built a few of these. This is as far as we ever got, though. We never actually put these into commercial production.

The next thing on Kiichiro's agenda was rockets. One day he dropped by, took out a one-hundred-yen bill—a denomination one didn't see too often back then—and told me: "Use this to buy all the books you can on rockets." I went over to Maruzen, one of Japan's biggest bookstores that is famous for its selection, and asked them: "Give me all the books you have on rockets." There could not have been even a dozen books on the subject, and all foreign at that. I brought these home with me and scoured them all for information. Every book I opened warned about the great dangers of experimenting with rockets. That spelled an end to that.

Kiichiro devoted himself to producing cars, but clearly must have been interested in many other things as well. He'd hear about one thing or other and have me study up on it. Of all these projects, the only one that reached some kind of tangible form was the helicopters that we test-built. However, our studies of airplanes and rockets were to be very helpful in our automaking efforts that would follow.

A MOTLEY CREW

Shibaura Laboratory was not an independent entity. It belonged to the Toyoda Automatic Loom Works, but no one was in charge on a day-to-day basis. Kiichiro had ultimate responsibility for the lab, but he showed up only once in a very rare while, so it was almost as if he weren't there at all. We all did pretty much as we pleased, working in a kind of purposive anarchy.

After me, the second to arrive at the lab was Hanji Umehara, a lecturer at Tohoku University whose specialty was thermodynamics. Kiichiro had asked him to study radiators. At first there were just the two of us, so I'd help out Umehara with his research and we'd go together to visit radiator plants.

I recall one dispute Umehara had with a master metalworker at a radiator plant we worked with. Umehara was a scholar. He had done all his calculations and claimed that a thickness of so many millimeters was ideal for cooling fins. But speaking from long years of experience, the metalworker, who was test-fabricating radiators for us, insisted on his opinion that the thinner the fins the more effective they would be. The two would stand there, arguing back and forth until they were blue in the face, neither giving an inch. Both had a point, but the fact of the matter was that radiator fins back then had not yet even been reduced to the thickness that Umehara had calculated. After the war, Umehara became a managing director of Toyota Motor Company, then was later appointed head of the Toyota Central Research & Development Laboratories, a facility that serves the entire Toyota Group.

The next to join the Shibaura Lab was a pilot by the name of Bunzaburo Kataoka. Kataoka was one of Japan's early aviators. I believe he had only three digits in his license number. He was always telling us stories. It seems that he had been with the *Asahi Shimbun* during the Kanto Earthquake of 1923. He told me that after the disaster, he had flown over Tokyo and seen large piles of corpses everywhere. On the first anniversary of the quake a year later, he took a priest from the Zojo-ji Temple in Tokyo up in his plane to pay respects to the dead. The priest chanted sutras right there in the plane. Kataoka explained that so many people had died in the earthquake that it would have been impossible for the priest to visit all the areas that had been hit by the disaster.

Then there was the story of how he had once pushed a geisha out of his plane. A spunky geisha in Shimbashi had said she wanted to try parachuting, so Kataoka took her up in the plane. Everything went fine until it came time to jump: she lost her nerve and wouldn't budge, so Kataoka pushed her out. Of course, she had her parachute on, but he said he was scared half out of his wits until he saw the parachute open. Kataoka, who was out of place at the lab, was there, I suspect, to pilot the little French plane that Kiichiro had bought.

Shisaburo Kurata, who later became a managing director of Toyoda Concrete, the precursor of Toyoda Soken, a manufacturer of concrete building materials, worked on remodeling the trucks Toyota was then making into four-wheel-drive vehicles. Before joining us at the lab, Kurata had been with Hakuyosha, a small automobile company that had been started in 1915 by people associated with the Mitsubishi *zaibatsu* and had since gone bankrupt. Shuji Ohno, later an executive vice president of Toyota, and Higuma Ikenaga, later a managing director of Toyota, also came over from Hakuyosha.

Kiichiro was totally caught up in auto development work. He asked Professor Kazuo Kumabe, a Todai classmate of his and later an executive vice president of Toyota, who was going on a trip abroad, to "bring back any interesting cars you find." Kumabe bought a German front-wheel-drive called the DKW and shipped it over to us. After driving this around for a while, we took it apart, then proceeded to test-build several cars based on it. I handled drawings of the engine, while Ikenaga made drawings of the chassis and other parts. It was the first time that drawings I made were transformed into a real car. The test-built cars were completed two years later. All told, we must have made about ten of them. These we drove, then took apart again to inspect and study some more.

We powered the cars with a two-cycle, two-cylinder engine, and both the engine and drive shaft were placed up front, as in today's front-engine, front-wheel-drive models. The body was made of wood and adorned with plywood and leather. This was nothing unusual back then, but it certainly looked a lot different from the cars we have today.

Another early member of the lab was Kichihei Miki, who was much older than the rest of us. When I first met him, Miki was an engineer at the Ministry of Commerce and Industry. Before that, he had been in the army, where he had done research on engines powered with alternative fuels such as charcoal and soybean oil. He joined us after retiring from the ministry and continued working on charcoal-fueled cars.

Back then, there were only four or five people in the machinery division at the ministry. Aside from Miki, the only other real engineer in the division was Ichibei Terazawa, who later served as an executive director of the organizing body for the Tokyo

International Motor Show. Terazawa single-handedly oversaw the entire Japanese machine industry. That just goes to show how bloated bureaucracy has gotten today.

Until Miki joined us, Toyota had no experts on charcoal-run vehicles. The technology for charcoal-powered cars was still immature and engineers were barely able to get them moving. I went once with Umehara to watch a demonstration in Osaka of a charcoal-driven bus someone had built. Unlike Tokyo, Osaka is fairly flat, so one thought that even a primitive charcoal-driven vehicle would have no problem negotiating the roads. As it turned out, however, the bus had a hard time making it up even the gentlest grades.

Miki made some initial improvements on charcoal-run vehicles, then later added more modifications during the war until these vehicles were running pretty well. Toyota improved the technology to the point where we were able to have a four-ton truck powered with charcoal pull another four-ton truck up the steep Hakone Mountains in test drives. This was no mean feat, I can assure you.

The Search for Parts

The Kariya assembly plant was completed and production of G1-type trucks begun in May 1936, the year Kiichiro had me set up the lab at Shibaura. Whenever I had time to spare, I would check out parts companies in Tokyo with Iwao Tatematsu, former chairman of Toyota Auto Body.

Logically speaking, it doesn't seem to make sense. We had already started production, so what were we doing hunting around for parts makers? After all, you can't make cars without parts. Actually, we were only able to get by because we were importing the parts we needed from the United States. We called the cars we were making Toyotas, but we depended on imports for all our electrical components, carburetors, speedometers, and even spark plugs. Putting this in a modern perspective, I wonder what the local content ratio was for those early Toyotas.

That is not to say that we weren't approached by domestic parts manufacturers. Companies such as Toshiba, Hitachi, and Fuji Electric were more than willing to make parts for us, but they had a hard time meeting our quality standards, and prices were inordinately high. Nippon Carburetor, to give one example, started making carburetors, so we agreed to use them, but they were priced much higher than the imports. Hitachi got wind of this and came over to make us an offer: "Listen, we're going to bring in technology from abroad and make these parts. Just give us your word that you'll buy them off us, okay?"

My job was to get hold of some reliable parts suppliers in the Tokyo district in time for the completion of the Koromo Plant (called the Honsha Plant today), which was still in the design stage over at headquarters. Back in 1936, the total lack of a parts industry as such was a major stumbling block to production. Without the parts you needed, things never went the way they were supposed to. A telegram from the plant would arrive each day at Kiichiro's home in Tokyo, telling him how many vehicles had been made that day. On some days, only one or two were made, on others none at all.

Circumstances among parts makers in Tokyo often defied belief. One local company let us know they were planning to start making meters, so I went over to have a look. I found a shop all right, but inside the place was empty except for some workbenches. No workers or equipment were to be seen. The president himself didn't seem to have a very good idea of how to make meters. Nor was this the worst. I heard of a place that manufactured meters, but when I went to pay them a visit, I found that the shop was located under an elevated railroad track. Every time a train passed overhead, the whole place shook like crazy. Any meters made here must have been totally worthless. Even so, this was a time when many small outfits like this made no bones about telling us that they were prepared to make meters.

One fairly decent parts maker was a place called Tokyo Sharin (now Topy Industries). They made products that rivaled imports in quality, probably because they had brought in Ford technology. Parts makers in Tokyo back then were clustered in Rokugo along National Route 1. I imagine that these served as suppliers for the assembly plant built by Ford-Japan in Yokohama. I wore down a lot of shoe leather touring that area.

Ford-Japan had a reputation back then for hiring workers at a starting wage of 5 yen a day. My salary was only 1.7 yen a day, and I had graduated from college, so Ford-Japan's wages were clearly high. The 5 yen attracted a lot of workers, but the company really worked them hard. Turnover was rapid because workers would wear themselves out before long and quit.

I also visited GM's assembly plant in Osaka. Shortly afterwards, Shotaro Kamiya, the former chairman of Toyota Motor Sales Company, came over to Toyota from GM. Kamiya was soon followed by two subordinates at GM: Seisi Kato, another former chairman of Toyota Motor Sales, U.S.A.; and Shikanosuke Hanasaki, a former managing director of Toyota Motor Sales.

THE PUSH FOR DOMESTIC PRODUCTION

In September 1936, a half-year after I joined Toyoda Automatic Loom Works, the company held an exhibition to commemorate the completion of what it called the "Toyoda Domestically Made People's Car" in Tokyo. I worked on the production of a public-relations film entitled *How a Car Is Made* for the exhibition. Naturally, there was no sound track, since "talkies" had hardly come onto the scene yet. It was the middle of summer, and I sat in a pitch-black room editing film and thinking about the narration to go along with it. We had a girl at the exhibition who read the script out to the audience as the movie was running. The film itself was shot entirely on location at our Kariya Plant.

Coinciding with the exhibition, the company decided on a new logo for its cars. Up until then, we had used the name "Toyoda," but that year we changed the *d* to a *t*, and in October the name officially became "Toyota."

At about the same time, the National Diet passed the Law Concerning the Manufacture of Motor Vehicles, under which Toyoda Automatic Loom Works was licensed to build cars and trucks. One problem the company had been faced with was how to respond to persistent demands by the government and military that it build domestic motor vehicles. The government had repeatedly exhorted Japanese concerns to move into vehicle production, but almost no one was willing to raise his hand and say: "We'll do it."

Then, just as the government was starting to think that it had no choice but to rely on GM and Ford, two men rose to the challenge: our Kiichiro and Nissan's Yoshisuke Ayukawa. They were called in by the government and told: "Now that Toyota and Nissan are starting to produce motor vehicles, tell us what support measures you'd like us to take." The responses made by Kiichiro and Ayukawa were essentially the same: "Government support measures up until now have been totally worthless. My company needs no assistance." Both argued that it was better to go it alone without aid from the government.

But could they afford to do so? Ford had an assembly plant in Yokohama and GM had one in Osaka. Both plants continued to run at full tilt, and Ford was even pondering plans to throw its momentum into the construction of a full-production facility in Kawasaki. Here Toyota and Nissan had at long last begun developing vehicles for domestic production, yet they were claiming to be able to get on without government support. Meanwhile, this overseas Goliath from Detroit was preparing to build a fully integrated facility in Japan. Clearly, the local companies didn't stand a chance. Something had to be done, but what?

Toyota and Nissan might go in and work for all they were worth, but they'd never catch up with GM and Ford. The solution the government came up with was to create the Law Concerning the Manufacture of Motor Vehicles to curb vehicle imports from abroad. The law provided, first of all, that companies manufacturing more than three thousand vehicles annually within Japan be licensed by the government. Secondly, it stipulated that a majority of the stockholders in such companies be imperial subjects. Clearly, the new law was aimed at restricting foreign capital.

Looking back on it now, this was a very low blow by the government against foreign automakers. In any case, following enactment of the new statute, Toyota and Nissan applied for permission to manufacture motor vehicles and were authorized to do so. The government had hoped that at least two companies would come forward in order that the principle of competition be kept alive within the industry, so it must have been relieved to see the enthusiastic reaction of Kiichiro and Ayukawa, two men obsessed with the automobile.

A high-ranking army officer once visited Kiichiro at his home under cover of darkness at the time the government was contemplating the creation of the law. I imagine that the army, knowing nothing about automaking and the auto industry, had sought Kiichiro's opinion on the matter.

The new law allowed GM and Ford to continue operating at their existing levels, but since both companies had already exceeded the annual production limit of three thousand units for unlicensed manufacturers, they were not permitted to increase their output any further.

IN AND OUT OF THE ARMY

I was transferred to company headquarters at Kariya in May 1937. They probably figured that I'd been taking it easy long enough in Tokyo and that it was time for me to get down to some real work. At Kariya, I was assigned to the Total Vehicle Engineering Administration Department, of which I was the only member. In a sense, Kiichiro had created the division specifically for me. My job was to resolve all the problems that users were filing complaints about. Although it was only my second year in the company, I was given full charge of this.

While at Kariya, I lived with Takeaki Shirai, former chairman of Nippondenso, and others at the company clubhouse. It was only a ten-minute walk to the plant, and we took all our meals at the company cafeteria. Since I was in charge of my own division, I didn't have to punch in at a time clock every day. Even so, I'd go in at seven in the morning and generally work until nine at night. My life revolved entirely around my work; the only time I returned to the clubhouse was to sleep.

The Marco Polo Bridge Incident occurred that July, just as I was at last getting used to my job. This minor clash in July between Japanese and Chinese troops near Peking triggered the Sino-Japanese War. The following month, I received a red draft notification slip inducting me into the service. I'd taken the military physical the summer before in Nagoya and been classified 1-B. When the war in China broke out, I was among the very first called up. Those drafted along with me who had military experience were immediately sent to the front, where they took part in the assault on Shanghai. A great many lost their lives there. I had no military experience, so I remained in Nagoya to receive training.

Because the military barracks were already packed to overflowing with soldiers headed for the front, we new recruits slept at a nearby grade school and were fed by families in the neighborhood. At first we had nothing to do other than eat and pass the time, so we had it good for a while.

I was assigned to a field artillery unit, where, obviously, we had to handle horses. Since the horses already there were being sent on to the war, local horses used to pull wagons and freight were rounded up as replacements. These horses were just as raw and inexperienced as those of us handling them. At first, the stables were full, so reed huts were set up at the center of the training grounds and the new horses kept there. The members of our unit took turns at "stable" duty. When your turn came, you had to stay up all night feeding the horses, cleaning out the stalls, and doing whatever else was called for, a routine that I found surprisingly rough.

When the main unit left for the front, the barracks emptied

out. We then moved over from the school and began our real training as artillerymen. The members of a field artillery unit should know how to handle both horses and cannon, but because this was a state of emergency, trainees in our unit were divided into two groups, placed in charge of either horses or ordnance, and drilled accordingly.

I was placed in the group handling ordnance. Cannon are relatively simple devices, so this was no problem at all. Draftees from farming families had strong backs and were able to lift heavy objects without difficulty, which I could not. On the other hand, I knew how to handle machinery, something they were unfamiliar with. The army gathered together people from all parts of the country, people of varied skills and background. But it was painfully clear to me that it was totally inept at making good use of the abilities of these draftees.

In October, I was suddenly discharged when a new military regulation was created stating, in effect, that individuals with technical skills essential to militarily vital industries should not be conscripted. Those who had already been drafted but were still able to return home were to be sent back. Afterwards, I learned from Kiichiro that a friend of his in the Army Ministry had told him about the new regulation and asked him: "Have you got anybody over at your company who falls into this category?" The first person that Kiichiro named was me. That's why I never went to the front.

I was in the army for two months. On August 18, just after I left for training, Toyota Motor Company was established by splitting off the automotive department of Toyoda Automatic Loom Works and setting it up as an independent entity. Since I was attached to the automotive department, my job remained the same as before I had been drafted. After being released from military service, I returned to live at the Kariya clubhouse and threw myself once more into my work.

In December of that year, production by Toyota finally reached the target of five hundred units a month we had set for the Kariya

Plant. Meanwhile, construction plans for the Koromo Plant continued to take shape. We had no time to lose, as demand for trucks climbed rapidly with the outbreak of hostilities in China.

Actually, for a short while, from the end of 1936 through early 1937, we had been unable to sell the vehicles we made. One reason, of course, was the depressed economy, but more importantly, our product just couldn't pass muster. The reason I was transferred to the Kariya Plant in May and placed in charge of product inspection and improvement was that, unless we were able to fix whatever was wrong with our cars and trucks, we would never be able to sell them. But more was required than just turning a bolt here and replacing a part there. And once we'd fixed whatever was wrong, we still had to go out there and regain the customer's confidence. If we failed to act promptly and effectively, the company would go under. It was as simple as that.

Or so we thought. The situation changed abruptly when the war in China broke out and the army bought up all our trucks, cleaning out our entire stock. Military procurements for the war were what saved the company.

THE KOROMO PLANT

The decision was made, at a Toyoda Automatic Loom Works board meeting in March 1937, to go ahead with both the establishment of Toyota Motor Company and construction of the Koromo Plant. For the meeting Kiichiro had prepared a paper entitled "Cost Accounting and Prospects for the Future," which he submitted to the board.

What he said in essence was that the sticker price on Ford and Chevrolet trucks was over 3,000 yen, so dealers were probably invoiced at about 2,800 yen. Naturally, Ford-Japan and GM-Japan turned a profit. Working backwards, this meant the cost of production was probably about 2,400 yen. If Toyota were able to make trucks for less than 2,400 yen and supply them to its dealers at 2,400 yen, the company could hold its own against Ford and GM. That was Toyota's initial target.

Production in October 1936 was 150 units, with this rising to 200 units in November. Based on these figures, production costs per vehicle came to 2,948 yen in October, and 2,761 yen in November. Since production capacity at the Kariya Plant was 500 vehicles per month, Kiichiro figured that at full production, costs would drop to 2,140 yen.

The Koromo Plant about to be built would have a monthly output of 1,500 vehicles, so assuming that this worked at full capacity and all products made were sold, production costs would fall to 1,850 yen. Supplying these vehicles to dealers at 2,400 yen would leave Toyota with a handsome profit.

According to Kiichiro's calculations, until all problems had been ironed out and the newly established company was fully up and running, it would incur losses of about one million yen through the first three fiscal half-year terms after incorporation. In the fourth half, facilities would be transferred to the newly completed Koromo Plant and operations begun. Full production right from the start would be out of the question, so output would initially be about 1,000 units a month. This would generate a profit of 1.2 million yen in the fourth half. In the fifth half, monthly production would be increased to 1,500 units, resulting in an output for that half of 9,000 vehicles. Profit for that fiscal term would amount to 1.8 million yen. In the sixth half, the company would pay out a dividend of 5 percent to its shareholders. At this rate, the company would be able to liquidate all its debts by the tenth half. That's the picture Kiichiro presented to the board.

Military procurements for the war in China helped Kiichiro's plans get off to a good start. Construction of the plant went smoothly and the company began massive hiring in spring 1938. I served as an instructor, teaching these new workers how to make cars. Many of those I taught lost their lives in the war, while others never came back to Toyota after the war. A goodly number, however, remained with the company until recently, working right on up until retirement.

We moved our facilities to the newly completed Koromo Plant

in the middle of summer, at the hottest time of the year. Most of the roads connecting Kariya and Koromo were inadequate for transporting heavy machinery, either because they were too narrow or the bridges too weak. What we did was select one route for carrying equipment to Koromo, and another for returning to the Kariya Plant. If we hadn't done this, trucks going in opposite directions would have met head-on somewhere and neither would have been able to get through.

I was in charge of the advance party. We received machinery delivered to Koromo and installed it at the designated locations. To decide on where to place the machinery, we drew a floor plan of the new plant with the equipment to be installed, based upon which we painted in the locations of the machinery directly on the plant floor.

Because the group sending out equipment at the Kariya Plant did so at its own convenience, the equipment usually arrived in Koromo at night. We had no lights at the new plant, so whenever a shipment arrived it was a disaster. I argued and pleaded with the people over at headquarters about this, and was somehow able to get the job done. The move left the plant idle for about a month.

At Koromo, we brought in production equipment that was still useful from Kariya and also installed new equipment. Some of this was imported from Europe and the U.S., but we also bought a great deal from domestic makers. For this reason, I spent a lot of time before the move visiting domestic machine tool makers to check whether they were capable of making equipment to our specifications.

Since we had already been licensed by the government to manufacture motor vehicles, I imagine that the equipment we imported from abroad was not subjected to import duties. In that sense, Toyota received government support. But the price of that support was having the government constantly breathing down our necks, pressuring us to get things rolling and increase our production capacity.

Following completion of the plant, we invited over a large number of associates and customers and held a big dedication ceremony on November third. That's why the anniversary of Toyota's founding is always held on this day rather than on August twenty-eighth, the day the company was actually founded.

SWITCHING OVER TO METRIC

While work was still in progress on the Koromo Plant, I led a task force to convert all our vehicle specs from the English yard-pound system to the metric system. Automakers in Japan had borrowed wholesale the system of measurement used in vehicles made in the United States, where, for example, the engine bore and stroke were given in inches.

Japan had ratified the metric convention in 1885, but the system did not take hold initially. Only now did the time become ripe for its use. That's why Toyota took advantage of the opportunity provided by the construction of the Koromo Plant to convert entirely to the metric system.

This may appear to be a simple matter, but in fact it was incredibly difficult. First, we had to replace all our machine tools, which were in inches, with metric tools. Then we had to redraw all our designs, a slow, laborious process that took a great deal of time and money.

What gave us the most trouble were screws. Until then, we had been using screws made to SAE (Society of Automobile Engineers) standards set in the U.S. Metric screw dimensions in Japan had been set by the Japan Engineering Standard, precursor to the current Japan Industrial Standard (JIS), but we were unable to use these without modification. We had to correct whatever was impractical or inconvenient and draw up new standards for automobile screws used at Toyota. This we did while referring to U.S.-made SAE screws. In fact, I did almost all of this work myself. The standards I set were later adopted as the official standards for Japan.

I believe Nissan continued with the yard-pound system until

the end of the war, probably because the exigencies of war production didn't allow them to switch over to metric. They seem to have gotten quite a lot of flak from the military over it too. Here Toyota was using the metric system while other makers were still working in pounds and yards. This meant that parts weren't interchangeable, which obviously created problems on the front.

Thus, although my main duties after being transferred to Kariya were product inspection and improvement, we were shorthanded, so I filled in wherever I was needed.

ROOTS OF THE *KANBAN* SYSTEM

Along with conversion to the metric system, it also had been decided to introduce a flow-production system at the new plant at Koromo. Even before construction of the plant began, Kiichiro had formulated a clear mental picture of the type of production system he wanted to set up. To help set up such a system, he put together a very detailed manual describing exactly what he had in mind.

At the Kariya Plant, castings for parts were stored temporarily in a warehouse, from which they were later taken as needed to be machined into the finished product. Each morning, slips were issued and circulated for each part, ordering the number of pistons, say, that were to be produced that day. After the pistons had been made, another slip would come by with instructions to bore holes in the pistons, and so on.

We were then using a lot production system, but Kiichiro's idea was to switch over entirely to a flow-type production system. He reasoned that this would eliminate large stocks of materials and parts, doing away with the need for warehouses. Cutting back running stock also would reduce capital outflow. If, once this production system got under way, we were able to sell our finished product before payments were due on our materials and parts, we would no longer have any need for operating capital.

What Kiichiro had in mind was to produce the needed quantity of the required parts each day. To make this a reality, every single step of the operation, like it or not, had to be converted over to his flow production system. Kiichiro referred to this as the "just-in-time" concept. By this he meant: "Just make what is needed in time, but don't make too much." We weren't even using the pallet cards called *kanban* at the time, but slips were passed around indicating the number of parts that had to be made or processed that day. If you finished early, you were free to go home early; if not, you put in overtime.

That was Kiichiro's idea in a nutshell, but how were we to put it into practice? The first thing that had to be done was give thorough training in the new method to the workers, or at least the foremen and shop supervisors. We were bringing in a radically new system. To get our people to accept it, we had to rid them entirely of their notions of the old way of doing things. It was, in a sense, a brainwashing operation. Kiichiro's manual was impressive. A full four inches thick, it described in meticulous detail the flow production system we were to set up. This is the text that I and the other instructors used to teach the new system to the workers. That marked the beginning of the Toyota production system. Ever since then, Toyota has used the term "just in time" to describe its system. Lately this has become something of a catchphrase even in the United States.

The system and its concepts that Kiichiro had taken such pains to teach and instill in Toyota workers was totally dismantled soon after the start of the war. Following the war, Taiichi Ohno, former executive vice president of Toyota, revived and further refined the system using the now legendary *kanban* cards.

With the completion of the Koromo Plant, I was placed in charge of the Second Machinery Shop. My job was to go onto the shop floor and put the production system Kiichiro had devised into practice. We had three machinery shops. The first made engines, the second engine accessories, and the third chassis components.

Each shop had three managers, of which one was responsible for inspection. Kiichiro's intention here was to catch any defective product and correct whatever processes were at fault. The task of the inspection manager was not simply to differentiate between a good and bad product, but to find a way to fix whatever had to be fixed—be it machinery, equipment, or tools—to prevent defective products from arising.

After the war, we studied quality control and actively incorporated this concept into our operations. The basic idea behind QC of "creating product quality within the process" is essentially identical to Kiichiro's thinking. This was an idea that would have occurred to anyone, and Kiichiro was certainly no genius for stumbling upon it. What set him apart was his initiative in putting the idea into practice.

GETTING MARRIED

In 1939, the year production at the Koromo Plant got fully under way, I agreed under my father's urging to a *miai*, a marriage meeting between prospective partners. I believe this was held on April 1—April Fool's Day. Six months later Kazuko and I were married. She was born in 1920, so she was seven years my junior.

Kazuko says that back when I was a fifth-grader listening to those early radio broadcasts in Nagoya with the crystal set I had built, she took part in some program or other, so I suppose there was a touch of destiny in our union.

Her father, Hansuke Takahashi, had been controller at Suzuki Shoten, one of the largest trading firms in the Taisho period (1912–26). Spurred on under the leadership of Naokichi Kaneko to catch up with and overtake the trading arms of the Mitsui and Mitsubishi *zaibatsu*, the firm at first underwent phenomenal growth but later collapsed during the financial crisis of 1927. My father-in-law was the Nagoya branch manager when the company went under. He stayed on in Nagoya and went into business for himself.

After our first encounter, I often went to visit Kazuko on my days off, but back then young people rarely had a chance to date alone. The only outing together that I can recall was our climb up Mt. Fuji that summer, and even then we weren't alone. My younger brother and a cousin also came along. We didn't get summer vacations at Toyota in those days, so after finishing work one Saturday evening, the four of us took a night train to the base of the mountain and started climbing the next morning. After reaching the summit in the early afternoon and resting for a short while, we started back down. We boarded a late train home and the next morning I was back at work as usual at seven o'clock.

Kazuko and I went to Kyushu for our honeymoon. We took the boat at Kobe, crossed the Inland Sea to Beppu, and, using that as our base camp, toured Mt. Aso and the Yabakei Gorge. Since I had been there once before in my university days, I was the guide. During our return trip, also by boat, Kazuko got a bit seasick the first night, but after that we had a calm and pleasant voyage.

Seeing that we needed somewhere to live, my father bought some land near the plant in Toyota City and built us a house there. The house was completed soon after the wedding, so I commuted from there to the plant in the early years of our marriage. (Today it is home to my eldest son, Kanshiro.) On my way to work each day, I passed through a small pine wood where edible *matsutake* mushrooms grew in the fall. I'd hide any mushrooms I spotted in the morning by covering them with grass, then pick them for dinner that evening on my way home.

TOYOTA–NISSAN–FORD: THE VENTURE THAT WASN'T MEANT TO BE

At about the time of my marriage, Toyota was faced with the problem of a possible partnership between domestic and foreign automakers. There was talk about Toyota, Nissan, and Ford possibly creating a joint venture in Japan. Kiichiro never mentioned the matter to me, so I had no idea what was really involved.

Then, a couple of years ago, evidence turned up that what we had heard had been more than just rumor. A venture had been in the making. At a party in spring 1984, the president of Ford-Japan approached me and said: "We found this document not too long ago when we were cleaning out our vault. I wonder if Toyota's got a copy too." When I replied that we didn't, he sent over a copy of the old agreement.

The three companies were to set up a joint venture in Japan, with Toyota and Nissan each putting up 30 percent of the capital, and Ford contributing a 40 percent share. The agreement, dated December 19, 1939, was signed by Nissan's Yoshisuke Ayukawa, Risaburo Toyoda (then president of Toyota), and Ford-Japan's Benjamin Copf.

I have my doubts as to whether Kiichiro was really in favor of this arrangement, but clearly talks had proceeded to quite an advanced stage. In July of that same year, he had told me and Shoichi Saito (chairman of Toyota Motor Company, 1972–78) to make a trip to the United States. I had no idea at the time why he wanted us to go to the U.S., but now that I think of it, it must have had something to do with the joint venture under consideration.

Kazuko was unhappy at the thought that my trip to the States might delay our marriage plans, but the decision had been made. With money the company had given me to make the necessary preparations, I had several suits made and reserved a berth for our crossing. Our friends at the plant even threw a big farewell party for us. Then, all of a sudden, just as the time had come for Saito and me to leave, everything was called off. The reason given was limited foreign-currency allocations. I imagine it was the military that intervened at the last minute.

I ended up with a lot of suits I didn't need and had a hard time facing all my friends after the grand send-off they had given us.

So I never made it to America that year, and the three-way merger between Toyota, Nissan, and Ford died a natural death as the storm clouds began to gather over relations between the U.S. and Japan.

AT WAR WITH THE U.S.

On the morning of December 8, 1941, I heard on the seven o'clock news that hostilities had broken out between Japan and the U.S. Ever since the beginning of the year, goods and materials had gotten harder and harder to come by. The sensation was one of growing discomfiture—sort of like being slowly suffocated. So news of the attack on Pearl Harbor brought mixed feelings; not that we knew whether we would win or not.

The actual situation, however, was much more serious than most of us suspected. I remember vividly how, when he heard the news of the hostilities, an elderly fellow by the name of Maruyama who had returned from the U.S. about a half-year before to work for Toyota uttered: "Japan doesn't stand a ghost of a chance." Most people were elated over the news of the Japanese attack, but Maruyama just sat there with his head in his hands, groaning: "We've gone and done it now."

I was neither very ecstatic nor expected that matters would become that grave. Although I did think the situation was very serious, I kept an optimistic outlook at first, expecting that things would probably work out somehow. In retrospect, however, it's quite clear that Japan's defeat was inevitable.

When war erupted between Japan and the U.S., Japan's annual production of crude steel was six million tons, equivalent to just twenty days of production by the U.S. That is all Japan was making when it started the war, and as the conflict intensified, steel production fell steadily.

Production figures were not reported to the public because the news was censored, but at Toyota we were keenly aware of the situation. Shortly before the end of the war, in 1945, annual production had fallen to a single day's output by the U.S. At that rate, it was no contest.

Just when I had become convinced that Japan would lose, the war came to an end and my second boy was born. As a reminder that we had lost the war because we had run plumb out of raw materials, especially iron, and could no longer continue to fight, I named my son Tetsuro. *Tetsu* means iron in Japanese.

Economic controls were first instituted in Japan while I was on a trip to China. Up until then, we had had a free economy, so when controls were suddenly imposed on us no one had any idea how to proceed. But because the law was the law, anyone caught in violation of the new regulations was arrested and punished. What had been permitted only yesterday was now forbidden, so the possibilities of breaking the law were infinite.

Shortly after I returned from China, Shuji Ohno, who later became an executive vice president of Toyota, was arrested and put in police custody on suspicion of some infraction or other. Neither Ohno nor those detaining him had any idea what it was all about. He was examined and soon released.

Once the war got under way, we entered a real wartime economy. Things were scarce, but because the economy was controlled, people would hide what they had. Of course, if you were found out, you were arrested. The regulations had been imposed to cope with material scarcities, but without materials we couldn't make products.

Nor were the government officials accustomed to the controls they were enforcing. So, as is to be expected, things didn't always go smoothly. Our operations were a perfect case in point. As an automaker, we couldn't very well build cars unless we received allotments of materials. We'd get orders from the military telling us to make so many trucks that month. Since material allotments came from one place and production orders from another, there was no way we could use the "just-in-time" system that we had developed with such care and effort.

With textiles, for example, it's easy enough to calculate how much thread or cloth can be made from a given amount of cotton. But trucks are a different matter entirely. Even with enough pig iron on hand for 10,000 trucks, if all you've got is 3,000 units' worth of sheet steel, you're only going to be able to turn out 3,000 vehicles. To make 10,000 trucks, you've got to have so many tons of pig iron and so many tons of sheet steel. Yet, adjustments of this sort are impossible in a controlled economy.

We had a hard time collecting the materials we needed for production. Under the controls, stockpiling of materials was a legal offense for which one could be arrested. But the army and navy were allowed to stockpile as much as they wanted, so we got what we needed from them. We figured that we had a right to those materials, since the vehicles we made were intended not only for the private market but for the military as well. However, when we went to the navy for pig iron, they'd tell us: "We've already given Toyota the pig iron it needs to build the trucks we ordered." If we then backed down, we'd never get the pig iron we wanted. So we'd try a different approach: "Look, you've given us the pig iron we need but we've got no sheet steel. Why don't you give us some extra pig iron. We'll trade that for sheet steel and build the trucks that you want."

The point of all this is that, if we had the materials, we could build the trucks somehow or other. I'd say, in fact, that when the war first began, most of our energy went into finding the materials we needed rather than building vehicles.

Toward the end of the war, practically any man who could carry a rifle and shoot was rounded up and sent out to the front. But there were always enough people around who couldn't go, so we never had any trouble gathering the manpower that we needed. At the close of the war, in addition to our regular employees, we had people from the army and navy working for us, as well as schoolchildren and townspeople—both men and women. There were nuns and geishas, and even convicted criminals.

Each of these people received different food rations. For some reason, however, the seasoned workers who labored the hardest and worked up the biggest appetites received the smallest rations, while the convicts were given the biggest portions. Irritated by the stupidity of this, I went over to the city hall to complain. But I was told simply that "the *Dajokan* decrees state that convicts get so many grams of rice per day."

Now that was going too far. These outdated laws had been issued more than a half-century earlier by the *Dajokan*, or Grand Council of State, a totally different system of government from what we now had. What in the world were these officials doing, talking about *Dajokan* decrees in the middle of a war? The people serving the rice really had trouble with that one. After all, there's no telling what someone who's famished may do. Try giving one person a heaping plate full of rice and skimping on the next guy's serving, then ask them to eat together and you'll have a fight on your hands over who was served how much.

Military call-ups took away most of our regular employees, but we managed to get by with local unskilled replacements and were able somehow to continue operating. Toyota's wartime production peaked in December 1941, when we put out two thousand vehicles, but dropped rapidly from 1942 on.

The Toyota Group Reorganizes

Toyota City, where Toyota headquarters is located today, was formerly called Koromo. The new plant at Koromo was built in 1938 at a place called Ronjigahara. When Toyota was in Kariya, the assembly plant was located near where the Kariya factory of Toyota Auto Body stands today. Following completion of the Koromo Plant, the company made truck cabs and rear decks at the Kariya assembly plant. These were built mostly from wood, so the place served as a woodworking shop, which required the use of only part of the entire plant.

As Japan fell deeper into war, it became harder and harder to get outside suppliers to make electrical components for us. We solved this shortage by starting to make the parts ourselves using the vacant space at the Kariya Plant. That parts plant has grown today into Nippondenso, Japan's largest manufacturer of electronic components for motor vehicles.

In addition to electrical parts, we also made tires at the Kariya Plant. Actually, this effort never got beyond the test-production stage, because the equipment at our tire plant was sent over to China. We transferred all our rubber technology to Tientsin but the staff remained behind, becoming the core of Toyoda Gosei.

The entire Toyota Group, including Toyoda Automatic Loom Works and Toyota Motor Corporation, has its roots in Toyoda Spinning & Weaving. But with the restructuring of the textile industry under the wartime controls, Toyoda Spinning & Weaving was merged with Utsumi Spinning & Weaving, Chuo Spinning & Weaving, Kyowa Spinning, and my father's company— Toyoda Oshikiri Spinning & Weaving—to form a single company called Chuo Spinning. This was done under a national decree to regroup companies in the textile and other industries into units of at least a minimum size, but as economic regulations were tightened even further, the textile industry was compelled to reform again into even larger groupings. Chuo Spinning then gave up all attempts to continue its spinning operations and merged with Toyota.

While this was going on, the army proposed that the Toyota Group, which was still shifting the core of its operations from loom-machinery production to truck manufacturing, start making aircraft. In order to fly planes, one first of all had to build engines. So we set up a company called Tokai Aircraft, with Toyota holding a 60 percent share and Kawasaki Aircraft supplying 40 percent of the investment. The new venture was to make powerful Benz V-12 engines that delivered more than 1,000 hp.

We needed machine tools to build the engines, so Kiichiro decided to erect a machine tool plant for Tokai Aircraft adjacent to the machine tool plant Toyoda Machine Works had at Kariya. A design was created that would allow cranes to join the two plants. I imagine that Kiichiro was prepared, if need be, to link operations at both plants.

Toyoda Machine Works became Toyota's first subsidiary in 1941 when the machine tool shop at Koromo was detached to form a company specializing in the production of machine tools for motor vehicle production. The new company supplied its products both to Toyota and to outside customers. Exercising its prerogative as an independent firm, the Machine Works decided to build a new plant on the north side of Toyota's Kariya assembly plant. Takatoshi Suga, who later became president of the company, was in charge of construction. I, too, was called on to help out, beginning with site selection. Although formally employed at Toyota, I worked at the Machine Works. Talk of Tokai Aircraft materialized just as the new plant was being completed.

Machine tools for mass-producing the aircraft engines were to be made near Toyoda Machine Works' new plant, but the plant for building the engines was to be constructed at a small airfield not far from the Koromo Plant that had been bought for this purpose.

Tokai Aircraft was to be set up as a privately owned company, but since it would be a "government policy concern" set up under state orders, the fixed assets—meaning the land on which it was built—were to be donated by the government. However, since the state needed more time to allocate the funds necessary for the purchase, Toyota bought the land up first. The state then bought the land back from Toyota, making it government-owned land, and donated it to Tokai Aircraft as the plant site.

This land was destined to remain in Toyota hands. After the war, the government sold it off to Toyota, which built the Motomachi Plant on the site. In other words, Toyota bought the same piece of land twice.

WARTIME INNOVATIONS

Facilities for the production of aircraft engines were completed at Tokai Aircraft's Kariya Plant and test runs started in 1944, by which time the tide of war had begun to turn unmistakably against Japan. But in 1945 Mitsubishi Heavy Industries' Nagoya works was destroyed by U.S. bombers, so the military had Mitsubishi move to Tokai Aircraft, driving us out. The military probably figured that it couldn't afford to wait any longer for us to build our souped-up Benz engines.

So it turned out that Tokai Aircraft's engines never saw the light of day. But the army also asked us during the war to build 500-hp star-type nine-cylinder engines for practice planes, which we did.

Just before the war ended, someone in the military decided to make a jet engine that the Germans were using, so the original plans were brought in from Germany by submarine. This jet engine consisted of three parts: a compressor, a combustion chamber, and a turbine. Toyota was assigned construction of the combustion chamber. We built a few of these, and I believe a couple of flights were even made by one plane that was equipped with this engine. But these ultimately played almost no part in the war.

During the war we experimented with more than just airplane engines. We also made quite a few unusual vehicles, mostly trucks. As raw materials became scarcer, the military had us build simple trucks using a bare minimum of materials. For example, toward the very end of the war, we were told that one headlight was enough and that we didn't need to install brakes on all four wheels—brakes on just the back wheels would do. Some of these trucks must have been downright dangerous to drive.

Under military orders, we also built an amphibious four-wheel-drive vehicle. Like any boat, this was propelled in the water by a screw. When it reached land, it would sort of ram into the shore and climb out of the water. This had to be a four-wheel-drive vehicle to travel over sand. We test-drove the vehicle on the banks of the Sumida River in Tokyo. All in all, the results were pretty good, so we built a number of these for military use.

We also came up with an unusual—to say the least—military truck that could be disassembled and backpacked across the mountains. When the troops reached a road again, they reassembled the truck and drove away. The frame was divided into sections and came apart by removing the bolts that held it together. These trucks actually saw use in remote parts of New Guinea.

We even made unmanned plywood boats that ran on truck engines. These were packed with explosives and launched at enemy ships. These contraptions ran at a speed of around 23 knots and could be fairly damaging when they hit their target; however, they were easily stopped by throwing logs into the water. The boats would run into these and, being made of just plywood, break up before reaching the enemy ships.

LAST DAYS OF THE WAR

A big earthquake hit the Tokai region where we were located in December 1944. This had the opposite effect of the Kamikaze, or "divine winds," typhoons that had saved Japan from the Mongol invasions in the thirteenth century. The earthquake crippled the local war effort; production of fighter planes in the Nagoya area was shut down.

When the quake struck, I was in Executive Vice President Hisayoshi Akai's office. We thought at first that we'd wait it out, but when the tremors got a bit too strong for comfort we rushed outdoors. It was so bad that all the water jumped out of the cisterns we were having built throughout the plant to douse flames in case a bombing raid was made against us. But since the epicenter was located quite a way off in the Kumano Sea, the Toyota plants weren't affected that badly. Local parts suppliers suffered considerable damage, however, on top of which the Tokaido railway, the main rail artery linking Nagoya with Tokyo and Osaka, was put out of commission for two weeks. A good deal of damage occurred along the eastern coastline, particularly at Fukuroi and Kakegawa, where many homes were destroyed and lives lost. Because the news was censored, however, we had no precise idea of the casualties.

The railroad being shut down for two weeks had the same effect as a railway strike. It practically paralyzed us, which was no surprise as this was the only widely available means of transportation back then. Of course, with the trucks we had, we were able to arrange for the delivery of parts from the Tokyo area, but we couldn't at the same time cover the delivery of materials to our suppliers. As a result, production was shut down for two weeks.

Another big quake hit in January 1945. This was a local, shallow-focus shock centered on nearby Mt. Sangane. Although the magnitude wasn't all that great, this quake caused quite a lot of damage in the immediate vicinity. The plant was largely spared, but some of our workers and their families suffered. Quite a few even perished. A large number of grade-schoolers from Nagoya who had been evacuated to the Mikawa area to escape the bombing raids on the city also died in that quake.

The second quake came late at night. We were sleeping at home, but had the windows open so that we could get out right away should there be an air raid. The children were asleep in a straw hut in the garden that a farmer in the neighborhood had built for us after the December quake. In a quake, a hut made of straw just crumbles and no one gets hurt.

In May 1945, just before the end of the war, I was made a director of the company on the recommendation of Akai. Kiichiro opposed my appointment. "Eiji's too young," he said. "Why he's only thirty or so." But that didn't deter Akai, who replied: "Age is of no concern in such matters." With his support, I was instated as a director.

Kiichiro had seen early on that Japan would suffer defeat at the hands of the U.S. and, losing interest in his work, spent the time immersed in his books. It was Akai who actually ran the company, but even he wasn't about to appoint directors without consulting the president.

Upon becoming a director, I served as manager of the delivery division, taking charge of the delivery of our finished trucks. Working with me as assistant manager was Seisi Kato.

After the war I learned that our plant had been marked as the

"Toyota Motor Factory" on U.S. aerial maps. We were spared initial attacks because the American forces hadn't included us on their hit list of vital plants.

U.S. planes strafed on a number of occasions, though. Japanese troops stationed next to the plant shot at some planes coming in, so the planes shot back. For some reason or other, they targeted the plant offices. Fortunately, Kato and I were out at the time. When we came back, our chairs had been shot to shreds.

The last bombing raid came on August 14, in the afternoon. Three B-29s each dropped a large bomb, either 500-kilo or one-tonners, I don't know which. The first bomb fell right next to the company housing complex, leaving a large crater. The second fell harmlessly into the Yahagi River nearby. But the third bomb fell right on the money, leveling about a quarter of the plant. Fortunately, in spite of the major damage to the plant, there were no casualties in the attack as all the workers had been evacuated following a strafing run that same morning.

I, too, had evacuated with the workers to a company shelter in the hills nearby, knowing that if an atomic bomb were dropped on the plant there'd be no hope of survival. A bomb of enormous destructive power had devastated Hiroshima a week earlier. When the Army General Staff Office announced that this was a new type of bomb that released high levels of radiation, I knew right away that they were talking about an A-bomb. I had read about the weapon in American journals before the war, so I had a general idea of how it worked. I also knew that it would be very difficult to make; therefore, when I learned that the U.S. had succeeded in developing the bomb in such a short time, I was amazed at the awesome powers of our foes.

After Japan's surrender on August 15, a bombing survey commission came to the plant to check on the effects of the air raid. They brought with them photos showing excellent aerial views of the plant. When I saw those pictures, I realized that there had been no way of evading an attack. The American forces had not bombed at random; they had taken careful aim.

I was horrified when I took a look at the bombing schedule the commission had with them. Toyota City was to have been bombed and burned to the ground exactly one week later, on August 21.

One bitter memory I have of the last days of the war was the death of Yoshito Hirahara. Just a couple of weeks earlier, I had sent Hirahara, who worked directly under me, on a business trip to Toyama. Although I explicitly told him not to stay overnight within the city itself, he failed to heed my warning. Unfortunately, the city was bombed that night and young Hirahara died in the raid. This was on August 2.

One other fellow who had gone along with him escaped harm. He left Hirahara's body in a safe spot and returned alone. Transportation was always a problem, but being a truck maker, we had means at our disposal, so we sent a truck out right away to Toyama. Hirahara was cremated at the Jintsu River in Toyama and his remains brought back to Toyota.

His parents lived in Hiroshima. There being no other way to get in touch with them, I sent someone out with news of their son's death. Before reaching Hiroshima, however, this fellow ran into an air raid, which delayed his arrival. Luckily for him he escaped the atomic bombing, arriving in Hiroshima immediately afterwards. But after taking one look at the devastation there, he became frightened and fled home. I then sent someone else out and was greatly relieved to learn that Hirahara's parents had escaped harm.

The war soon ended and the funeral was held shortly thereafter. It was difficult for me to get over the fact that I had, in a sense, sent Hirahara to his death, a death that was hardly honorable as the war was already almost over.

His son is alive and well today, working at Toyota.

Having heard that the emperor was to make an announcement at noon on August 15, we all gathered around the radio in the office at the appointed hour. A lieutenant standing beside me, who had been stationed at the plant as an inspector, was having trouble understanding the broadcast.

"What's he saying? What's the emperor saying?" he asked me.

When I answered that the emperor had announced he was calling an end to the war, the lieutenant turned aside in disgust and returned to his office.

That morning, all the workers had climbed onto the roof of the plant to clear it of broken slate from the air raid the day before. Some continued working until about three o'clock in the afternoon because it took time for word of the emperor's broadcast to be transmitted to everyone. However, by nightfall, news that the war was over had spread throughout the entire plant. Everyone was stunned. Unable to go on with their restoration work, they stopped what they were doing and went home.

The next day, on the sixteenth, a number of problems emerged. We had a large number of workers at the plant. Now that the war was over, many were saying that they wanted to return to their families. Local people who had been compelled by the authorities to work at the plant presented no problem because they were not there of their own choosing. Women students and junior high schoolers who had come from a distance were staying in the dormitories and, although the war had ended, would be unable to return home except in groups.

But no one had any money to pay for the trip home. Not that it made much difference. Even had they had enough for train fare, the railroads were totally disrupted. There were soldiers, too, who wanted to return to their units but were unable to do so right away. The company would have to make arrangements for the smooth return home of its workers.

Those helping out the employees returning home were busy, but the rest of us didn't quite know what to do with ourselves. We came to the office out of force of habit, but instead of working we just sat around blankly, asking each other what would happen when the American troops arrived. That was the biggest concern on all of our minds. What would happen next?

After lunch, Akai assembled all the managers in the dining room and gave us a pep talk. "We lost the war," he began. "But mark my words, in five years we'll be back on our feet again. The trucks that Toyota makes may have been vital to the war effort, but they're going to be just as important in rebuilding Japan. Toyota has a responsibility to make and supply those trucks, so let's start over once again with that in mind."

Akai's speech fired everyone up. We had shut down our operations on the fifteenth—the day after the bombing—and on the sixteenth we all agreed to resume production the following day.

Those who had to return home began to do so in droves on the seventeenth. A few days later, the close to ten thousand workers at the plant had dwindled to our three thousand regular employees. With so many people gone, the place became a little desolate. But we were fortunate in one sense: had all ten thousand remained behind, we would have had to feed them, and there was little around to feed them with. Now that most of the work force had left, we were able to live for a while off the stocks of food we had, which relieved us of some of the immediate concern of finding food.

I forget how many vehicles were built on the seventeenth, but we abandoned the wartime specs for trucks with just one headlamp and brakes on only the rear wheels. From that point on, all the trucks we made had brakes on all four wheels, and a pair of headlights.

During the general confusion that marked the last months of the war, I was in charge of product delivery. Under the economic controls, sales and marketing activities were nonexistent; all we had to do was deliver the goods into the hands of the buyer.

The army and navy units stationed near the plant would sometimes come to us asking for truck parts. Of course, formal procedures for requisitioning parts existed, but these took too long, so they'd come directly to us, since we were in the neighborhood. This was in clear violation of the regulations, but as someone once said: "Necessity knows no laws." Handing over the parts was a violation on our part as well, but how can you refuse someone who comes to you in need?

We were willing to hand over some of our spare parts, but weren't about to give them away free. Although we expected to be paid for the parts, the army and navy just dragged their feet. When the war ended, I told my staff: "Once the units are dispersed we'll never get our money. It's now or never." We hurried over and made the military write out checks to us. But the units broke up spontaneously with the end of the war and the surrender, and the checks were never honored.

Part 3

Picking Up the Pieces

NEW LINES OF WORK

I don't recall what Kiichiro was doing when the war ended, but one day at the end of August he came over to the plant and made a speech.

"It's all well and good to build trucks as Akai says, but there's no knowing how long we'll be able to keep at it under a military occupation. We've got several thousand employees and their families to look after. The very first thing we ought to do is think about how we're going to give these people work and keep them fed."

Here's what Kiichiro proposed that Toyota do. The basic material needs are food, clothing, and shelter. No one, occupation army included, was going to tell us not to make and supply these three essentials. The problem was what exactly we should produce. Since we had run a textile company, this was an obvious choice. We had the skills and technology, and could dive right in at any time. So much for clothing. That left food and shelter to worry about.

Kiichiro ordered me to set up a chinaware franchise. Even if we weren't allowed to make trucks or cars, we'd be able to get by dealing in china. That was the reasoning. Kiichiro told me to set up ties with ceramics makers in the nearby Seto district, famous for its glazed ceramic ware.

Another idea of his was to make fish paste. Shoichiro, Kiichiro's eldest son and today the president of Toyota, even went to the city of Wakkanai in northern Hokkaido and began making fish paste there. Kiichiro also thought of raising loaches, a small eel-like freshwater fish, as a source of much-needed protein. He had Shoichi Saito (former chairman of Toyota) go and discuss the idea with a professor at Kyoto University.

I imagine Kiichiro had foreseen the defeat of Japan and, to prepare for the inevitable, had come up with these ideas for new businesses. In any case, he soon had a lot of people moving on them.

As it turned out, however, following talks with the occupation army the following month, we were given permission to build trucks and buses, although cars were out of the question. Kiichiro's new enterprises were soon abandoned. The only one that was continued was the production of concrete for housing projects. This has become Toyoda Soken, today a supplier of one of Toyota's prefabricated houses.

Once truck production had been formally okayed by the occupation command, we set up an internal reconstruction office to coordinate repairs on the damaged plant, and immediately began to design and test-produce vehicles. In just a year and a half, we were able to bring out our first postwar trucks.

DEATH OF THE VICE PRESIDENT

Executive Vice President Akai, who had cheered and encouraged us with his assurances that Toyota would fully recover within five years, died in a traffic accident one cold day in December 1945.

He had spent several days at Toyoda Automatic Loom Works in Kariya. On the day of the accident, some cranks that we had ordered from the Loom Works were taking forever to arrive, so I, too, headed for Kariya to hurry things up a bit. At the Loom Works, I met first with Taizo Ishida and listened to his explanation for the delay. The company had contracted out the cranks to a parts outfit in Handa, a nearby city, so I went over myself to check on how work was progressing.

I raised a bit of hell at Handa, then started back for headquarters. On my way to Koromo, however, I came upon one of our company cars stopped by the side of the road. When I asked what the problem was, the driver told me that a kingpin had broken and the car wouldn't budge.

Busted kingpins were commonplace in those days. I handed the driver a spare I had and he set to work on it. It turned out that Akai had been riding in the car. According to the driver, a truck from the Loom Works had stopped by the stalled car and taken Akai on to Koromo.

Sakichi Toyoda (1867–1930), Japan's "King of Inventors" and the founding father of the Toyota Group.

Kiichiro Toyoda (1894–1952), the founder of Toyota Motor Company.

Risaburo Toyoda (1884–1952), the first president of Toyota Motor Company.

Taizo Ishida (1888-1979), who was appointed president of Toyota Motor Company following the labor dispute in 1950 and who played an important role in the company's reconstruction.

The author (*second from right at the back*) with members of the First Middle School of Aichi Kendo Club, 1926.

The author (*center rear*) and other recipients of the West Prize for mechanical engineering pose after graduation in front of the Charles Dickinson West statue. (March 1935)

Sakichi's automatic loom. Sales of the patent rights to Platt Brothers of England provided the seed money for Kiichiro's new venture—automobiles.

Shotaro Kamiya (*second from left*) shows off Toyoda's new AA sedan at the "Toyoda Domestically Made People's Car" exhibition held in Tokyo on September 14, 1936. Risaburo Toyoda is standing at the back, extreme right.

The author with Bunzaburo Kataoka, a pilot hired by Kiichiro. (Around 1936)

The author and his future wife, Kazuko Takahashi, together with the author's younger brother and a cousin, resting during a climb of Mt. Fuji. (Summer, 1939)

Toyota Motor Company's new Koromo Plant nearing completion sometime in early 1938.

The author (*center right*) in Beijing. (September 1940)

Between November 1943 and August 1944, Toyota built 198 four-wheel-drive amphibious vehicles on the orders of the military. Here is one being tested in late 1943.

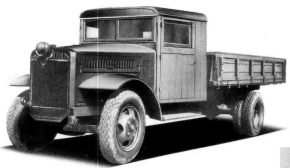

In an attempt to conserve dwindling supplies during the last days of the World War II, some trucks, including the KC model shown here, were made with only one headlight and no front brakes.

Following talks with the U.S. occupation forces, Toyota was formally given the go-ahead to resume bus and truck production in December 1945.

Nagoya City during an air raid by U.S. B29 bombers in March 1945.

The Toyota SA, or the "Toyopet" as it came to be known, was introduced in 1947 as the first result of Toyota's research into the popular economy car. It is shown here racing the "Tsubame" express as part of a domestic advertising campaign.

The negotiations during the 1950 labor dispute.

A union rally in the 1950 labor dispute.

Exports of trucks like these to U.N. and U.S. forces in Korea helped Toyota's reconstruction after near-collapse in 1950. Such exports came to an abrupt end in 1962 when the U.S. Congress passed a law requiring the military to buy only trucks made in the United States.

Toasting the first Crown to roll off the line at Toyota's new Motomachi Plant are members of Toyota Motor Company (*left*) and Toyota Motor Sales (*right*). The author is third from the extreme left. To his left is Executive Vice President Fukio Nakagawa. (1959)

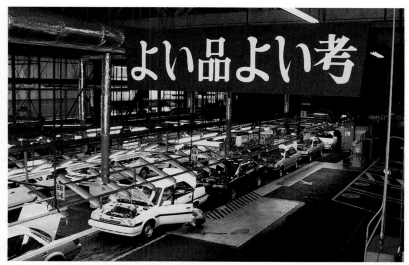

"Good Thinking, Good Products," which has been Toyota's motto since March 1953, appears here and throughout the company's many facilities.

One result of the author's visit to Ford in 1950 was the introduction of an employee-suggestion system. Shown here is the first poster calling for employee participation.

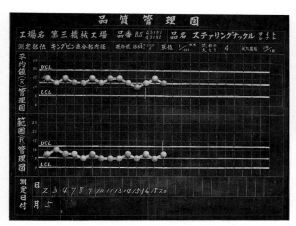

Statistical quality control was introduced into all aspects of Toyota's operations in May 1953. This early chart mapping daily fluctuations in production quality is for steering knuckles.

The author shows the Crown assembly line to the Crown Prince (*second from left*) at the Koromo Plant. (March 1955)

Toyota's DA60 diesel truck was marketed from March 1957.

Toyota's first exports to the U.S., two Crowns, wait to be loaded at Yokohama in August 1957.

Her Imperial Highness Empress Nagako speaks with the president of Toyota Motor Company, Taizo Ishida, during a 1957 visit by the emperor and empress to the Koromo Plant. The author looks on from behind.

The headquarters of Toyota Motor Sales, U.S.A., in California as it looked in its early days.

Entering the market six months after arch-rival Nissan's popular "Sunny" (Sentra), the Corolla appealed to buyers by emphasizing its "extra 100cc" of power. The ad campaign was far more successful than anticipated.

Toyota Central Research & Development Laboratories, established in November 1960, as they appear today from the air.

The author with the president of Toyota Motor Sales, Shotaro Kamiya, at the ceremony marking Toyota's tie-up with Daihatsu Motor in 1967.

The author addresses a special session of the Japanese Diet as an expert witness on the emissions control issue in September 1974.

The author with James
Hirata (*center*), who helped
him such a lot on his 1950
visit to Ford, and former
Toyota Motor Company
chairman Shoichi Saito
(*left*) at the Motomachi
Plant. (August 1977)

The author with Ford chairman Henry Ford II during
his visit to Toyota in 1978.
On four occasions talks between the two companies
have taken place but without
any results.

The two Toyotas decided to merge in 1982. (*From left*) Masaya
Hanai, the chairman of Toyota Motor Company; the author, then
president; Shoichiro Toyoda, president of Toyota Motor Sales;
and Seisi Kato, chairman of Toyota Motor Sales.

The author with GM chairman Roger Smith in April 1984 at the Toyota Kaikan Exhibition Hall in Toyota City.

The author and Shoichiro Toyoda greeting U.S. ambassador Mike Mansfield at a reception held in 1982 to mark their appointment to chairman and president, respectively, of the newly formed Toyota Motor Corporation.

The author and Willem H. Welling, executive director of the Bernard van Leer Foundation, discuss the future of private grant-making foundations over dinner as part of a 1984 international symposium sponsored by the Toyota Foundation in celebration of its tenth anniversary.

The author addressing a group of graduates of the Toyota Technological Institute in March 1986.

But as I learned shortly, the truck carrying Akai had rolled over into a rice paddy on the way back to headquarters. I arrived at the scene of the accident soon afterwards. Two people were lying down on the back of a rescue truck. One was a young fellow at Toyota by the name of Wakamatsu, and the other was Masao Naruse, a professor at Tohoku University. Wakamatsu was a student of Naruse's.

"Professor Naruse," I called out, not sure whether I would get a response. The first thing he asked me was: "How's Wakamatsu?" He was more concerned about his student than himself.

But there was no sign of Akai. I figured that he had already been taken to the hospital by the rescue squad. Of course, I was concerned about Akai, but first I had to take a good look at the scene of the accident. I noticed an impression in the mud that looked exactly as if it had been made by someone's head. That's when I realized that Akai had probably banged up his head. Later, when I went over to the hospital, I learned that he was already dead.

Kiichiro and Risaburo rushed over to the hospital. Ishida arrived later than the others, perhaps because he hadn't heard the news right away. The moment he saw Ishida, Risaburo thundered: "You killed Akai!" This took Ishida completely by surprise. He didn't even know yet that a truck from the Loom Works had been responsible for the mishap.

But how in the world had all this happened? Professor Naruse later told me that they had visited Akai's home that day and talk had turned to the vice president's son. I don't know all the details, but the two had later gone over to see his son's teacher, who lived in Okazaki. Afterwards, Akai and the professor had stopped by Toyoda Machine Works in Kariya, and from there had headed for Koromo. That's when the car in which they were riding broke down. When a truck from the Loom Works came by and offered them a lift, although it was a cold day, instead of riding in the cab, Akai, the professor, and Wakamatsu hopped onto the back of the truck.

The road on which the accident occurred had some tricky stretches full of sharp curves. The driver of the truck, knowing full well the dangers and aware that he was carrying a top Toyota executive, apparently intended to take a longer but safer route. But having countless times driven over dangerous roads himself, Akai told the driver to take the shorter route. The mishap occurred when the driver cut too sharply at a sudden turn, landing the truck in a rice paddy.

According to Naruse, the truck tipped over to the right, throwing the riders at the back into the paddy and landing on top of them. When the truck started rolling, Naruse flung himself as far away as he could. That's what saved him. Akai, however, was pinned under the truck, and young Wakamatsu also died shortly after the accident.

Some time later, Kiichiro brought over a professor at Tokyo University, Kazuo Kumabe, as Akai's successor to the vice presidency. Professor Kumabe was a close friend of Kiichiro's and a gifted scholar, but was not, unfortunately, at home in the world of corporate management.

The Labor Union Law was enacted shortly after Akai's death. With the establishment of this new law, I realized that it would be just a matter of time before a labor union arose at Toyota. Since this was inevitable, it was clear that we should have people who understood the company's viewpoint play a key role in organizing such a union. The Toyota Motor Koromo Labor Union was thus set up in 1946 with cooperation from the company. But with the poor economic conditions that racked those early postwar years, the union grew increasingly radical as time passed.

Relations between labor and management began to deteriorate at about the time Kumabe was appointed executive vice president. Had Akai been alive, he would have handled this in a businesslike manner, but Kumabe resorted to idealistic arguments. I can't help feeling that if Akai had not met with that accident, affairs at Toyota might have turned out very differently.

A New Dealer Network Is Born

Immediately after the end of the war, the General Headquarters of the Allied Powers, or GHQ as everyone called it, spelled out an occupation policy that included the abolition of wartime economic regulations.

Motor vehicle sales during the war were conducted under a rationing system operated by a nationwide wholesaler called the Japan Motorcar Distribution System with prefectural distributorships serving as local retailers. Dealers for Toyota and Nissan had been lumped together early in the war into local vehicle distribution companies.

After the war, however, the GHQ ordered an end to this monopolistic, centrally controlled system. Without these distribution companies, Toyota would be stripped of its sales channels. We had to act fast and set up new channels at once. Shotaro Kamiya, who had served as a managing director of the Motorcar Distribution System, took the lead in building up Toyota's sales network.

The dissolution of the wartime distribution companies had left local dealers out in the cold wondering what to do next. Kamiya rapidly made the rounds of local distribution companies throughout Japan, persuading them to join Toyota. Thanks to his efforts, most of the local distribution companies came over to us. We got to work on this a lot faster than Nissan, and the early advantages this gave us probably have a lot to do with why we continue today to enjoy a lead over Nissan in domestic sales.

The regional distribution companies set up during the war were essentially formed by grouping together local dealerships in the respective prefectures. These were headed by people who had been dealers for Toyota, Nissan, or Isuzu before the war, but Kamiya managed to draw many dealers who had been with Nissan into the Toyota fold. As a result, even today, there still are a good number of Toyota dealers around who worked for Nissan before the war.

Kamiya's efforts failed to pay off only in Tokyo and Osaka. The president of the Tokyo organization had been a Toyota man, but he crossed over to Nissan. As for Osaka, the number one man there had been a dealer for Nissan, while the number two man had worked with Toyota. Ultimately, after intense recruiting efforts by both sides, the heads at these two distributorships chose to join the Nissan network. The death of the vice president at Osaka also played a hand in eroding support there for Toyota. The repercussions have continued to this day. That is one reason why Toyota's share of the Tokyo and Osaka markets today is lower than our national average.

It was certainly no easy process, but the rapid establishment of a national sales network immediately after the end of the war owes a great deal to Kamiya's energetic efforts.

AT THE BRINK OF FAILURE

Production in number of units was hardly better in 1946 than 1945, mainly on account of material shortages, not poor sales. Means of transportation were limited, so it's conceivable that we could have sold anything we made, but the buyers had no money. If you're unable to collect payment after a sale, that hardly amounts to a sale. This problem continued to plague us for a long time and eventually brought Toyota to the verge of bankruptcy.

Here we were, then, unable to turn out vehicles as we wanted when the millions of soldiers and civilians who had fought and worked in Japan's overseas territories came pouring home. The first thing these repatriates needed were jobs.

We continued our chinaware ventures, but Kiichiro really had his heart in cars and trucks. It occurred to us that by contracting business from the U.S. occupation forces, we'd be able to continue working with vehicles and at the same time be assured of payment. So we began taking on repair work at our plant in Kariya, where we had been making aircraft engines. Since that wasn't enough to get by on, however, we also opened up some dry-cleaning establishments.

Just as work was beginning to go smoothly at last, talk of war reparations arose. Military industries that had been making aircraft and ordnance were the first registered for reparations. Our plants were next on the list, but we fought to have these excluded because if our equipment were seized, this would have destroyed any hope we had for recovery.

Then Toyota was targeted under the Deconcentration Law, passed by the Japanese Diet in 1947 under pressure from MacArthur to dissolve excessive concentrations of economic power. We succeeded in having our name struck from this list as well, but eventually fell under a SCAP (Supreme Command for the Allied Powers) directive on "Restricted Concerns." This compelled us, under the Enterprise Reconstruction and Reorganization Plan, to detach Nippondenso and Toyoda Spinning & Weaving as independent companies.

While all this was going on, severe inflation ravaged the economy in 1947. This got so bad that at one point we were raising wages every month just to stay even. Occupation authorities had decreed, moreover, that pay increases for directors of "restricted concerns" were not to be allowed. That's why we received the lowest wages in the company.

Not only had my salary dwindled to practically nothing, the stock I owned in the company was non-dividend-paying, so we got no income from this either. I think I had about two thousand company shares in my name, but since I had bought these with loans, I had interest to pay off. We had some savings, but with assets frozen, these were out of our reach. Without some form of cash income, how were we to make ends meet? Although she never came right out and said so, I know my wife had a hard time getting us through those days.

The deflationary measures known as the "Dodge Line" were instituted in 1948, and the following year the Shoup mission issued its recommendations for reforming Japan's tax system. Although the Dodge Line was successful in curbing inflation, it threw the country into a deep recession. The effect this had on Toyota was to make it impossible for us to collect payments on the trucks we had sold. Most of our sales were on an installment basis, which meant that buyers had an easy time meeting payments during times of inflation. But when we were hit suddenly with deflation precipitated by the new economic measures, many buyers found themselves unable to meet the installments. Since even those who were honest and well-intentioned were unable to pay, clearly the less scrupulous buyers weren't about to do so either. Without money flowing back to the company, we were unable to pay out wages.

This was at a time when labor unrest and agitation was breaking out at quite a number of companies. Any attempt by management to cut back on personnel would have met with fierce union resistance and possibly a strike, so we didn't see this as an option readily open to us. Toyota managed to scrape by somehow through the fall of 1949, but wages were being paid over a month behind schedule. Things got so bad that we wondered whether we'd be able to make it through the end of the year. We were desperate, so we ran around trying to collect from any buyers who looked as if they could pay up. Unfortunately, we didn't have much success.

My father, Heikichi, died on October 18, 1949, just as the recession was at its worst. Toyota stock had fallen below par value to forty-eight yen per share. As soon as my father died, the revenue office began badgering me to pay off the inheritance taxes. I inherited Toyota stock from my father, but no money to pay the taxes. The only thing I could do was pay with the shares I had inherited.

Inheritance taxes are assessed based on the value of assets at the time of death. I paid the taxes in kind because by that time the value of Toyota stock had plunged to twenty-seven yen, about half of par value, so that cashing in my shares would have meant taking a loss.

Thus, both I and the company were dead poor at the time. But worse was to come.

In 1950, we hit a cash flow crunch right around New Year's. It would be just a matter of time before we went broke. Things had gone as far as they could possibly go. That's when help arrived. Takeo Takanashi, then head of the Bank of Japan's Nagoya district office and later chairman of Tokyo Toyopet, Toyota's largest domestic dealer, gathered together representatives from a number of banks and told them bluntly: "I want you to do something for Toyota." This saved the company, but the assistance came with some strings attached: we would have to make substantial personnel cuts and split off our sales department as an independent concern.

Takanashi did what he could for us because he realized that a great number of peripheral industries were tied to the auto industry. He knew that if Toyota folded, this would have very broad repercussions. Without his help, there's no question that we would have gone under. Toyota owes a great debt of gratitude indeed to Takanashi.

Faced with the very real threat of bankruptcy, we began in early 1950 to put together a plan for getting the company back on its feet. We laid our proposal, which included cutting the work force by 1,600 people, before the union in April. This sparked a furor among the membership that led to a succession of strikes, work stoppages, and mass protests over the next two months.

Just before the labor dispute finally subsided in June, Kiichiro went before the assembled members of the union. "Much as I'm against it," he told them, "unless we make these cuts, the company doesn't stand a chance." Then, in a tearful voice, he announced: "I'm personally taking responsibility for this by quitting." With that, he resigned.

Taizo Ishida came over from Toyoda Automatic Loom Works as the new president, and Fukio Nakagawa of the Mitsui Bank was appointed senior managing director to oversee financial reorganization of the company. Next in the chain of command was Shuji Ohno, followed by me.

I, too, was a target of harsh questioning and denunciation by the union at the time of these layoffs. As head of the Engineering Department, I once had to face two thousand workers filled with hostility toward me. "Toyota is like a boat that is foundering." I said. "Unless someone jumps off into the water, the boat will sink. That's why I want you to recognize the need for personnel cuts."

Photos of that day are still on display at the union hall. The reply by the union was: "No way! Call off the cuts!" But since a company works on cold economic principles, there's no room for emotion in a situation like this. Some understand this more easily than others, however.

It was not the banks that appointed Ishida president. One day, at the height of the debate over the layoffs, Risaburo Toyoda, Kiichiro, Ishida, and I met at Risaburo's home in Nagoya. Kiichiro turned to Ishida. "I want you to take over for me," he said. "How about it?"

"If that's what you want, then I will," replied Ishida. And that's how it was decided.

Toyoda Automatic Loom Works, which Ishida was then president of, was doing very well. One weaver who used the company's automatic looms had even said: "All you've got to do is run this machinery once and you're ten thousand yen richer." Kiichiro reasoned that if Ishida, as president of the prospering Loom Works, were also appointed president of Toyota, this would win back confidence in the company. He believed also that the banks would probably go along with this arrangement.

Ishida maintained later on that the move had been of his own doing. The way he explained it, "If Toyota had gone under, no matter how good business was for the Loom Works, we would have been hit by the aftershocks and maybe even dragged under along with Toyota. That's why I had no choice but to step in."

He had a point there. The Loom Works may have been doing very well just then, but the bankruptcy of Toyota would have been a severe blow to it. Ishida felt that, at the very least, he should do whatever possible to protect the Loom Works. This is probably why he and Risaburo were able to see eye to eye on the matter.

Ishida knew hardly anything about cars when he became president of Toyota. The Loom Works had made parts for us on two occasions while he was at the helm there. The first time had been at the outset of the Pacific War. Loom manufacture was a peacetime industry, so even if the company received orders for looms, it wasn't allocated the materials to build them. Kiichiro decided to contract some of Toyota's work out to the Loom Works, so Ishida came over with several of his staff one day, chose what he wanted to do, and returned home with some parts orders.

After the war ended, the Loom Works again took parts orders from us for a while to fill the gap left by the ordnance work it had been doing during the war. But when the loom business began picking up again, they gave this up. I imagine that the way Ishida saw it was: "There's nothing around less profitable than making trucks."

When the sales department was split off from Toyota Motor Company (TMC) in April 1950 and incorporated as the Toyota Motor Sales Company (TMS), Shotaro Kamiya resigned from TMC to become president of TMS. Having been designated a "restricted concern," Toyota was not allowed to own stock in a company detached from it. This was tantamount to throwing TMS out naked into the freezing cold. The new company, while granted exclusive sales rights for Toyota, was permitted no overt financial connections with TMC.

This situation left us uneasy, however, so we indirectly bought and held stock in TMS. We had done the same with Nippondenso and Toyoda Spinning & Weaving, which we had been forced to split off earlier. These moves were not always strictly legal, of course, but it was a time when strict observance of the law was not always the right thing to do.

Once the labor dispute had been settled, a special stockholders' meeting was held in July at which Ishida was appointed president and I was appointed a managing director. I didn't attend the meeting because I had left for the United States as soon as the strike was over.

Going to the U.S. in those days was no simple matter. I was shocked to learn that instead of "Japanese," my passport listed me as "Japanese under Directive No. XX of the Supreme Commander for the Allied Powers" and gave my race as "Mongoloid." Under the occupation, Japan was not treated as a fully sovereign nation.

The purpose of my visit to the U.S. was to gauge the future prospects of the auto industry and to explore the possibility of arranging for technical cooperation of some sort from U.S. manufacturers. Having decided that it would be in our best interest to establish ties with American automakers, we sent a proposal to Ford, with whom we had previously entered into negotiations.

Kamiya had gone over earlier to open up talks and arrange for simple technical guidance. I was to follow in order to conclude the negotiations and sign the agreement, but on the eve of my departure the Korean War broke out. One clause of the agreement called for Ford to send us some engineers, but the U.S. government issued an injunction forbidding valuable technical personnel from leaving the country, which put an end to that. However, since this outcome was not of Ford's making, they agreed to receive trainees from Toyota. Kamiya returned to Japan soon after concluding the agreement.

STATESIDE

In July, I left for the United States, where I stayed for three months. I studied at Ford for the first month and a half and visited machine tool makers at various points in the U.S. during the remainder of my stay. An associate by the name of Weaver who had been in charge of machinery transactions at Mitsui & Co.'s

New York branch office before the war served as my guarantor during my stay in the U.S.

When I visited Ford, the founder of the company, Henry Ford I, had died three years earlier and his grandson, Henry Ford II, had taken over as president. Calling his grandfather's ways "old-fashioned and outmoded," the younger Ford set out to modernize management totally. Shortly after the war, he brought in a group of young, talented scholars and put together a new management to carry into effect his grand vision.

I learned a great deal from this group of fresh talent. The folks who had been with the company since the first Henry Ford went around with this look on their faces that said: "What in the hell can *they* do, anyway?" But these young "whiz kids" were working directly under the big boss, who, in addition to being new around the place himself, was only in his thirties. So they were riding high and mighty. Those days were a period of transition for Ford as well.

At any rate, I learned a great number of things at Ford. The day I arrived at the company headquarters in Dearborn, the first thing I was asked was: "What is it you want to study here?"

"Quality control, production methods, the works," I answered, telling the staff member everything I had in mind.

He looked at me in surprise. "Hold on, there. You want to know too much," he said. "To begin with, nobody at Ford knows everything that goes on around here."

"Maybe so," I thought to myself. "Maybe you don't have anyone like that at Ford, but we do at Toyota." Of course, that's not the sort of thing you come right out and say, so I just held my peace.

The first class I attended was on budgetary management. It was part of a training course offered to new staff members at the company. Although I listened carefully, I couldn't catch anything of what was being said, so I passed on this after one day. I then went to a lecture on quality control but had a hard time following this as well.

The moment I stepped into a factory, however, I was back in familiar territory. The first plant I visited at Ford, the River Rouge Plant, had two assembly lines and turned out about one vehicle a minute, or some 800 units daily. The cars being made there were the first postwar models. Both the engines and transmissions were the same as in the prewar models; only the body had been modified somewhat. Yet, since supply during the war had come to a standstill, Ford was selling even its old models as fast as they could turn them out. The company as a whole had a daily output of about 8,000 units, so the River Rouge Plant accounted for about 10 percent of the total. In addition to vehicle assembly, this enormous facility also made engines and other components for supply to other assembly plants.

I was supposed to undergo hands-on training at the River Rouge Plant, but I didn't do any work to speak of. Instead, I spent most of my time simply wandering around, observing and asking people working there all sorts of questions. They were always glad to explain to me what they knew.

I also visited the Highland Park Plant, where Model T Fords had been made before the war, the spanking new Mound Road Plant, a forging plant near Goodyear Tire and Rubber, a carburetor plant, a piston ring plant, a bearing plant, and even a valve lifter plant.

At the Mound Road Plant, I took a week-long training course on automatic transmissions with people from Ford dealerships around the world during which we actually took the transmissions apart and reassembled them again. Cars with automatic transmissions had just come out and Ford was in the process of putting together a training manual on these. We were the guinea pigs on which the usefulness of the new manual was being tested.

Our group was broken up into teams of two each. I was paired up with a fellow from Israel, but trainees had arrived also from such places as France, Argentina, and Spain.

On the last evening of the course, we had a farewell bash. First we boozed it up awhile at the hotel where we were staying, then went out on the town in a couple of cars and dropped by a Chinese restaurant for some food. I turned out to be the only one who knew how to use chopsticks, so I showed everyone else how it was done. Then we continued drinking and carousing around town late into the night.

I visited just about all of the Ford plants in and around Detroit, but, wanting to take a comparative look at the facilities at other automakers as well, I also toured an automobile plant and a truck plant at Chrysler.

Although I didn't have an opportunity to see any of GM's plants, based on what I'd seen at the plants I did visit, I remember thinking: "Detroit isn't doing anything Toyota doesn't already know." Of course, when Toyota began making cars before the war, it had taken a good look at what automakers were doing in America. I'd arrived in Detroit with some background knowledge, and what I saw while I was there convinced me that, because little progress had been made during the war, the information that I had remained for the most part valid.

After my return to Japan, I was often asked: "How many years before we catch up with Ford?" To tell the truth, there was no way of knowing. I felt that I was being honest in saying: "Ford's not doing anything we don't already know." But at the same time I was certainly not presumptuously downplaying Ford's tremendous lead. After all, their daily output was 8,000 units; ours was a piddling 40. You might as well compare a pebble with a boulder. In terms of corporate size, we were in very different leagues. Yet, I didn't think that there was such a large gap in technology. The difference lay mainly in the scale of production. I felt that if the size of Toyota's operations grew large enough, we'd be fully able to handle an American-type production system.

While in Detroit, I stayed at a place called the Dearborn Inn. This was a hotel that had been built by Ford and was located on an immense tract of Ford land. The company treated me handsomely while I was in Detroit, sending out a car to take me wherever I had to go, be it the hotel, company headquarters, or a plant. I was even allowed to take my lunches in the executive dining room.

The person who had arranged all this for me at Ford was James Hirata. About sixty-five at the time, he worked as a consultant in either the inspection or precision measurement department—I don't recall exactly which. I imagine that the reason he had the time to look after me was because he had retired from the front line of activity.

Hirata had a colorful past. It was interesting just to hear him talk about it. He was born in Japan, the third son of a farmer in Gifu Prefecture. While he was still in his early teens, his father told him: "Go out and find yourself some work." He was given a little money to tide him over the first few days and practically kicked out of the house. Young Hirata, still wet behind the ears, decided to strike off for America and go into business for himself.

The only way to get over to the United States was by ship. Ships for the U.S. departed from Yokohama, so that's where he headed first. It took him a while, but after a few months of working and traveling, he arrived in the port city. Once there, he swam out to a freighter anchored offshore and talked the captain into letting him work on board. I don't know if his ploy worked the first time through, but he landed himself a job as a cabin boy and, three years after sailing out of Yokohama, managed to reach San Francisco.

When he arrived in America, construction was in progress on the transcontinental railroad, so he joined a railway crew and gradually worked his way east. He got as far as Detroit, where, by some stroke of good fortune, Henry Ford I took him under his wing and even sent him off to school.

During the war, he was supposed to have been placed in a relocation camp, but Ford intervened, telling the authorities that Hirata was an important engineer and keeping him at the company. However, since he was too conspicuous to remain at headquarters, Hirata was sent to work in a subsidiary for the duration of the war. After the end of the war, he returned to the head company. In any case, Hirata had gotten himself into the good graces of Ford senior.

When I met him, Hirata had trouble speaking Japanese, probably because it had been decades since he had last spoken with anyone from Japan. He even took me golfing during my stay in Detroit. This was the start of a long friendship. I later visited him at his home in Florida following his retirement, and Hirata came to visit me twice in Japan. He died several years ago at the age of ninety-five.

I spent six weeks in Detroit, then for the remaining month and a half I traveled around, visiting machine tool makers. After stopping at two or three plants in Detroit, I went on to Cleveland, Cincinnati, and Rochester. Machine tool plants were also scattered throughout much of lower New England—Connecticut, Rhode Island, and Massachusetts. One place I visited was a machine tool maker located in Providence, Rhode Island.

During this period, I stayed at a hotel in New York City. On weekdays, I'd ride the train and bus, dropping by maybe two or three plants. Then on weekends I returned to New York. I followed this same routine for a number of weeks. It's not that I had anything important to do in New York; I just had nowhere else in particular to go.

In addition to which, I had little money. Before leaving Japan, I'd been given a foreign currency allocation of three thousand dollars, but after paying for my round-trip airfare and all the expenses of my journey, this left nothing over for extras. The plane tickets alone came to a little over one thousand dollars, so I had very little spending money during my stay. I had enough to pay for my hotel accommodations in New York, but that was it. Since I couldn't afford to eat all my meals in the hotel, I just ate breakfast there and went across the street to a Chinese restaurant for lunch and supper.

I suppose I could have used up the two thousand dollars left over after subtracting the airfare, but I had to have something in reserve in case I got sick. Back then, I knew absolutely no one in New York, and there certainly wasn't anyone around who would lend me some money if I needed it. That's why I lived frugally during those weeks in New York, making sure I always had a little cash to spare.

Having nothing better to do on the weekends, I'd pass the time by visiting the Metropolitan Museum of Art, walking over to Central Park, or simply riding the subway. You could ride the New York subway anywhere for the price of a token. So, for example, I'd ride all the way to the last station on the line. If I found a zoo there, say, I'd visit that. Then I'd get back on again and ride all the way in the other direction. Once, I got off the subway at the southern tip of Manhattan just as a ferry was about to depart, so I hopped on board without knowing where it was headed. I now realize that this took me to Staten Island, but since I didn't have any idea at the time where I was, I took the next ferry back. Time after time, I acted the part of the country bumpkin out for a tour of the big city.

In October, Shoichi Saito arrived from Japan and took over for me, so I headed back home.

SPECIAL PROCUREMENTS: A HELPING HAND

Military procurements by the U.N. and American forces in Korea provided Toyota with a solution to its reconstruction efforts. During the strike, we had drawn up a plan for rebuilding the company based on a monthly production limited to 960 units and had pared our work force accordingly. But just as we were getting ready to put this plan into action, the Korean War broke out. We received large-volume orders for trucks from the U.S. military, which had decided to buy from Japan because trucks delivered from the States would be too expensive and would never make it in time for the war.

The U.S. military continued to buy from us for over ten years, even after the end of the Korean War. Procurements stopped abruptly in 1962 because the U.S. Congress passed a law stating that American forces had to buy trucks made in America. Some congressman from Michigan attached a rider stating in effect that "the U.S. Armed Forces shall not buy Japanese-made trucks" onto an unrelated bill that had just passed through a congressional committee.

Of course, the U.S. military didn't know anything about this until it was too late. It only found out about the rider after the law had been passed before a full session of Congress. They got pretty upset about it, but there was nothing they could do. This happened while I was on an economic mission to the U.S. When I learned what had happened, I changed my plans and rushed over to Washington, where I filed complaints with the State Department and the Department of the Treasury. "What's the idea of cancelling orders made under contract without so much as a warning?" I asked. "That's a funny way to do business."

At first, trucks bought by the U.S. military in Japan were put into service in Korea, but later procurements were used for supplying military aid to U.S. allies in Southeast Asia, such as the Philippines, Thailand, Indonesia, and South Vietnam. The result, of course, was high profits for Japanese manufacturers. In fact, business got so good that Citibank even set up a branch office for Toyota right in Nagoya, in the hope of cashing in on these special procurements.

In spite of the strike, the layoffs, and everything else that had occurred that year, when we closed the books for the half from April to September 1950—our twenty-second fiscal term—we had zero profits and zero losses. The only reason we were able to break even during that difficult six-month period was because of a reassessment of our assets. Then, in our twenty-third term, with the new business that the special procurements represented, not only did the company register a net profit, it was even able to pay out a dividend for the first time in seven years. What had driven Toyota to the tottering edge of bankruptcy had been the losses in irrecoverable payments incurred from our installment sales. But now, with the military procurements, we knew that our payments would be honored because we were dealing with the U.S. government. Why, we were even allowed to raise our prices!

This was truly a gift from heaven. Our cash flow situation improved immensely. With the extra money we soon had on hand, we also were able to put more muscle into our domestic sales. Management began to change course and head off in the right direction. Although Ishida's efforts had a lot to do with the success of Toyota's recovery, the luck that he brought with him played an even greater part.

Soon after my return to Japan, payment for the procurements had not come in yet, so management got together and discussed what internal changes the company should be making that didn't require an input of cash. We decided then and there that we could streamline operations and cut transportation costs. Both could be accomplished without further expenditures. All we had to do was use our know-how. While at Ford, I had seen how considerable savings in manpower could be had in materials handling by judiciously making even minor changes, so we decided to begin there. That's how Toyota's suggestion system got started.

A LAST TRIBUTE TO KIICHIRO AND RISABURO

Cash flow eased up considerably in 1951, so we began to pipe some of our profits back into research and development. With Ishida continually expanding Toyota's capital during this period, money poured in from both the capital increases and profits. As a result of this, our balance sheet improved dramatically.

With the company's general financial picture now brighter, Ishida asked Kiichiro to come back and take over once again. This was in early 1952. Perhaps out of embarrassment, Kiichiro was at first reluctant. "An automaker that doesn't make cars is no automaker at all," he said. "I don't have any intention of running such a company."

With some coaxing, however, Ishida eventually won him over.

"When you come back," he told Kiichiro, "you can have the company start making passenger cars." With that, the decision was made to reinstate Kiichiro as president of Toyota.

Once this had been decided, Kiichiro himself got fired up and raring to go. Then tragedy hit. On March 27, he died suddenly of a stroke. He was only fifty-seven and still had some of his best years ahead of him. I strongly suspect that what killed him may have been the intense excitement he felt at the thought of returning to the company.

So Ishida continued as president. Then, two months later, on June 3, Risaburo, the first president of Toyota, also passed away. He was sixty-eight.

Because he was already bedridden from illness when Kiichiro died, Risaburo had been unable to attend Kiichiro's funeral. I went to his home in Nagoya to give an account of the ceremony. While I was there he moaned from his bed: "Whatever you do, have Toyota make cars." The one person who had been the most opposed to Toyota making passenger cars was spurring us on from his deathbed. "Toyota should no longer be making just trucks," Risaburo was saying. "Whatever you do, go out and make passenger cars!"

"We're getting ready to start passenger car production right now," I said. "Just make sure you're around to see us begin." But Risaburo passed away just a few weeks later.

Kiichiro and Risaburo differed in every way possible—their personalities, their sense of responsibility, and even what they stood for. Kiichiro had this "Toyota is mine" attitude. He felt that Toyota had been given to him by his father, Sakichi, that "we built Toyota, so we can tear it down again."

On the other hand, Risaburo had an abiding sense of mission. His attitude was: "My father-in-law, Sakichi, entrusted Toyota to me. My duty is to make the business grow and prosper." Unlike Kiichiro, there was no question in his mind of tearing Toyota down and returning it to a cipher.

Their basic attitudes were totally irreconcilable. Anyone coming between the two would only get it from both sides.

Risaburo would get furious at times. Even I had come on the receiving end of his wrath. But at the same time he was also an extremely considerate and generous soul.

Kiichiro, on the other hand, rarely complimented people. He griped at me constantly, but that's probably because I was close to him. Rarely did he complain to those who came from outside the Toyota circle. He never let down that guard right up to the very end.

I suppose that Kiichiro's ways rubbed off on me, because at the company I do nothing but complain: I hardly ever pay anyone a compliment. It seems that the closer one is to one's subordinates, the easier it is to gripe.

Part 4

The Road to the Top

Toyota Begins Making Cars

When Kiichiro first went into the car business, he dreamed of one day making and supplying to the people of Japan passenger cars that held their own with the Fords and Chevys, economy cars for the average family that incorporated all the latest technology. He was trying to abide by the words of his father, Sakichi: "Stay ahead of the times."

Toyota began research on a popular economy car shortly after the end of the war. At the same time, the company also initiated the test-production of small trucks, and it was these which it put out on the market first. We started to research passenger cars in earnest at the end of 1945 when the GHQ authorized the commercial production of vehicles for the general public. Throughout those turbulent early postwar years, buffeted by inflation, deflation, and labor unrest, we continued without interruption to study passenger cars.

In 1947, just two years after the end of the war, we announced our model SA, a small passenger car that we affectionately called the "Toyopet." Then, in October 1951, we brought out the Toyopet SF sedan, an improvised vehicle created essentially by mounting a car body onto a truck chassis. We sold the SF for use as a taxi. Back then, even "taxi-trucks" were in high demand in Japan.

We had three different suppliers make sedan bodies for the SF: Mitsubishi Heavy Industries in Nagoya, Kanto Auto Works, and Arakawa Auto Body. While buying time with such expedients, we continued to make steady progress toward the production of a "real" passenger car.

Our first true passenger car was the Crown, unveiled in January 1955. In fact, the first Crown actually rolled off the assembly line in a ceremony held on New Year's Day. Because I had been involved in this project from the development stage, I attended the ceremony in a tuxedo and drove the first car off the line.

Shortly thereafter, we completed a prototype of the Crown Deluxe. On March 30, Crown Prince Akihito came to visit the Koromo Plant. While giving him a tour of the plant, I said on impulse: "We've completed a deluxe version of the Crown. Would Your Highness care to take it for a drive?"

"Yes, I certainly would," he replied. So, with the prince at the wheel and me in the passenger seat next to him, we made a circuit of the factory. I had forgotten to ask him whether he had a driver's license or not, but he really knew how to drive, which was for me, considering the circumstances, completely unnerving. The only problem was that he floored the thing. We launched the Crown Deluxe that same December.

Two years later, in April 1957, Emperor Hirohito and Empress Nagako also visited the plant. Ishida was at the head of the procession with the emperor, explaining everything to His Majesty. The empress came next, followed by me. Concerned lest Ishida make a mistake, I tried to get as close to him as possible, but was reprimanded by members of the Imperial Household Agency and told not to approach so closely to Her Highness.

Coming as they did just as our reconstruction efforts were getting under full steam, these visits by the crown prince and the royal couple were truly an undeserved honor for Toyota.

The Crown was very well received in Japan, so we decided to try selling it in the United States. In October 1957, we established Toyota Motor Sales, U.S.A. Our entry into the overseas market might have looked as if it were smooth sailing all the way, but in fact it wasn't.

European cars had been making inroads in the U.S. market since about 1955, and the best-selling foreign car was Volkswagen of West Germany. At one time European cars had close to a 10 percent share of the American car market. We saw all too well that at this rate America would eventually rise up in anger against foreign "intrusion" in its markets.

Watching all this from Japan, Shotaro Kamiya, then president of Toyota Motor Sales, mused: "If the U.S. goes ahead and restricts imports, Toyota will be cut out of the American market for good. We've got to get in there now or never." That was the situation as we saw it, so we loaded a couple of Crowns on a ship and sent them over.

Although the Crown was doing well in Japan, we didn't have the slightest idea how it would fare over in the States. All we knew for certain was that once import restrictions were erected, any hope we had of exporting to the U.S. would vanish, regardless of how good our product was. There were no two ways about it; we had to get a foot in the door.

It's commonly believed that we exported because we had confidence in our product. But, if anything, our exports to the U.S. were attributable to Kamiya's foresight and his infallible marketing instincts.

So we took our chances and began exporting to the U.S. in order to "stake our claim." But the reception was horrible. To begin with, the car didn't have enough power to travel on high-speed roads. In retrospect, that first initiative of ours was very poorly thought out indeed, but our timing was definitely not off. In fact, having this bitter experience behind us helped us work that much harder afterwards to build cars that were right for the U.S. market.

The pressure was on. Unless we exported a "decent" car as soon as we possibly could, this would spell an end to Toyota Motor Sales, U.S.A. For us, it was "do or die." We had to come through now or forever abandon our ambitions for the U.S. market.

To have succeeded then and there in rebuilding Toyota, U.S.A., would have given us the happy ending we were all hoping for. Unfortunately, as it turned out, our American franchise almost collapsed a little later, forcing us to trim the staff and reduce the scale of operations. I myself flew over to handle the dismissals.

Ishida remained president of Toyoda Automatic Loom Works even after his appointment as president of Toyota, so he was acting CEO of both companies. But when he talked of "my company," he was referring to the Loom Works. That's where his real loyalties lay. Right up until his very death, Ishida always thought of Toyoda as "the world's number-one loom maker." To him, the auto business was more or less just a sideline.

At first, he was a rank amateur when it came to cars, but he applied himself and learned a great deal. When we chose the radiator grille design for the first Crown model, Ishida came over and we all discussed the matter together. He ended up deciding on a roundish design that resembled a pair of glasses, and this went over quite well with the customers.

Ishida had a knack for resolving sticky conflicts. Once, in 1954—the year before we launched the Crown—I was trying to get a plan approved for the construction of a building for the Engineering Division, but Executive Vice President Nakagawa refused to okay it. At Ishida's suggestion, we reduced the height of the first floor by a foot and this time got Nakagawa's approval.

Ishida recognized the need for the building but wasn't about to override Nakagawa's objection at the risk of humiliating him. By having us cut a foot from the height of the building, Ishida enabled him to accept my proposal without losing face. Whenever I was at odds with Nakagawa, Ishida generally backed me up.

In September 1954, we marketed the SKB, a small, one-ton, cab-over truck. Earlier that year, during the New Year's season, I had to go to Brazil and Mexico on business. I left, telling my people in the Engineering Department: "I want you to finish building prototypes of the SKB by the time I return in early March." That's why the first SKB prototypes were made in just two months. The manager of the Engineering Division at the time was none other than Hanji Umehara, with whom I'd worked at our little lab in

Shibaura shortly after entering Toyoda Automatic Loom Works in 1936.

The goal we had set for the SKB was to take over the market for three-wheeled trucks. Most trucks back then were three-wheelers. We developed a small, low-priced four-wheeler and marketed it to the hilt. The SKB, launched that September, did even better than we had expected. Within no time at all it literally put to rout three-wheeled trucks, giving us the results we sought.

In 1957, we also launched the Corona, which was somewhat smaller than the Crown and powered by a smaller engine. Engine displacement was 1500cc in the Crown and just 1000cc in the Corona.

Up until 1955, sales of Toyota vehicles were all handled by a single "Toyota" dealer network. But as the number of our models increased, this setup grew more and more inadequate, so we decided to try having multiple franchises handle separately the local sales of different Toyota models. Today, a multiple dealer system is the norm, but back in those days it was a bold marketing idea. We were breaking totally new ground. Existing dealers were dead set against the idea, claiming that the new outlets would infringe on their rights. Under the one-dealer, one-prefecture system we had relied on up until then, a single dealer had exclusive rights to the sale of Toyota vehicles in an entire prefecture. However, the new arrangement meant that other franchises selling Toyota products would be opening up shop in the same territory.

Kamiya did all he could to convince Toyota dealers around the country that this was for the best, and in 1956, after overcoming much resistance, we set up the Toyopet franchise. At last, the multiple dealer system was a reality. The first product sold at these new dealerships was our small SKB truck. To help along sales of the SKB, we renamed it the Toyoace shortly after the Toyopet outlets were opened. Just as the name implied, we were hoping that this would come through for us like a true ace.

Then, in 1957, we set up a third dealer network: a franchise for diesel products. Toyota had begun test-building diesel-powered vehicles around 1955 and commercially marketed its first diesel truck in 1957. This event was surrounded by considerable controversy. The way the government saw it, Isuzu Motors had already starting making diesel-powered vehicles, so there was no call for Nissan and Toyota to jump in as well.

The Ministry of Trade and Industry (MITI) called me in, and an official in the Heavy Industry Bureau told me point-blank to have Toyota call off its sales of diesel trucks. This was too much. "The government has no right to tell us to stop," I retorted. "Toyota will continue selling diesel trucks even if the ministry is against it."

To drive the point home, we deliberately set up the diesel franchise. But demand for diesel-powered vehicles was still very low, so we opened only about nine outlets in Tokyo, Osaka, and Nagoya. Our existing "Toyota" dealerships handled sales of diesel products in other areas. These several diesel outlets served as the foundation for our Publica franchise, which later became our Corolla dealer network.

THE MOTOMACHI PLANT

Despite our best efforts, exports of the Crown to the U.S. were a continuing source of frustration and disappointment. But on the home market, demand grew steadily, not only for taxis, but also for commercial-use vehicles and company fleets. Business got so brisk that we were barely able to keep up with orders. That's when I suggested to Ishida that we build a new plant for the production of passenger cars.

Thinking ahead to the future, I wanted to propose that we construct a plant that could handle the production of 10,000 vehicles a month, but this was a mind-boggling figure back then. Even though the Crown was moving well domestically, sales still barely topped 2,000 units a month. Unless demand went on growing, such a large plant would be working at less than 30 percent of capacity. So I proposed instead a facility that would turn out

5,000 units. Even a plant of this size was a risky venture.

Ishida, who was by now beginning to feel more at home and self-confident in his role as president of an automaker, made the final decision on construction of the plant. Even looking back on it after all these years, this was an important decision. We set up an internal plant construction committee in July 1958, and immediately began drawing up plans for erecting the enormous facility.

Shoichiro Toyoda was appointed head of the committee, and I acted as supervisor. Before we began actual construction of our new facility—which we named the Motomachi Plant, Shoichiro traveled to Europe and looked over a number of plants, including the Renault plant in France which had recently been completed. This was actually made up of three smaller plants—a body shop, a painting shop, and an assembly shop.

The plant was completed in August 1959. Although we installed the facilities and equipment needed for a monthly output of 5,000 vehicles, we had built enough additional floor space to allow production to be expanded to 10,000 units. This decision was made by Ishida, and for once Nakagawa said nothing.

In September, we held a huge dedication ceremony, inviting over a large number of people, including MITI officials, industry leaders such as Katsuji Kawamata of Nissan Motors and Isuzu Motors' Naomichi Kusunoki, not to mention people from our dealer organizations. Back then, it was common practice to invite over other industry people on such occasions. We were more generous and open-minded with each other. Vehicle makers had worked hard together during the war, so we knew each other well. We were on good terms, not at each other's throats.

Kusunoki couldn't hide his amazement. "Toyota has really gone and done it now," he said.

Our dealers got scared. "How are we ever going to be able to sell all the cars you make at such a big plant?" they asked. "This is going too far."

Soon after the ceremony, we were hit by a large typhoon. Had the Motomachi Plant been completed just a little bit later, this storm would have caused heavy damage and considerably delayed the opening. Fortunately for us, damage at the plant was slight, but facilities owned by many of our suppliers in the Nagoya area were hurt badly. The sea rose right up to the Nagoya railway station. Many parts of the city are located at sea level, so once seawater comes in, it takes a long time to recede. First, embankments were built, then the water pumped out, so it took about half a year for water to be cleared out of the city entirely.

Things quieted down within about two weeks at the Motomachi Plant, so we brought in equipment from our suppliers who were unable to continue production until the waters had receded, set this up in our empty shops, and had parts made for us right there. Aichi Prefecture was hit very hard by the typhoon, but Toyota managed somehow to escape major damage.

After a while, everything settled back down to normal again, and in December of that year, the company as a whole finally reached a production level of 10,000 units per month. In addition to the Honsha Plant with its output of 5,000 units, we had built a new plant capable of turning out an additional 5,000 vehicles and had it operating at full capacity in a matter of months.

The Motomachi Plant was built at a time of intense capital investment that preceded the rapid expansion of the Japanese economy in the early 1960s. If we were to build a plant that size today, it would probably call for an investment of 400–500 billion yen or more. The excellent timing of this plant was another good example of Ishida's unique blend of luck and intuition.

More than a quarter of a century has passed since the Motomachi Plant was built. Some additions and renovations have been made over the years, and today it puts out 13,000 Crowns a month. Combined with cars from the Mark II series, total plant production is 30,000 units a month.

Original construction costs were covered by expanding capital and taking out loans. Although profits continued to roll in from the military procurements, Toyota was still basically a poor company. In that sense, construction of the plant was a big gamble that would either pay off handsomely or ruin us. Had we lost the gamble, we probably would have fallen on hard times again.

With Ishida's decision to go ahead and build the plant, Toyota suddenly rose head and shoulders above its domestic competitors. Until then, the local industry had been like a tournament of midgets. Nissan's Oppama Plant and Isuzu's Fujisawa Plant were completed several years later, in 1962, by which time we had already finished second-phase construction at Motomachi.

So we gained a decisive edge right from the start. Ever since then, we've continually pressed on for fear of being overtaken, rapidly putting up one new factory after another—Kamigo, Takaoka, Tsutsumi—to keep pace with the wave of motorization that hit Japan in the 1960s. By that time, we had won the confidence of the banks and no longer had difficulty raising capital or securing loans for new construction.

As for my part in all of this, I took the initiative in building the Crown. At a time when other Japanese automakers were enlisting help from overseas partners to begin the production of passenger cars, Toyota relied solely on itself. The fact that we developed and produced the Crown entirely by ourselves won us widespread support and helped get us going smoothly on our way. It's probably no exaggeration to say that Toyota developed into what it is today largely because of the Crown.

After making sure that the Motomachi Plant got off to a successful start, Ishida resigned as company president in August 1961. He then became chairman and Nakagawa was appointed his successor without much ado. At the time of his retirement, Ishida was already seventy-six and felt that turning things over to me would be too large a jump down in age, so he settled on Nakagawa, who was midway between the two of us.

When Nakagawa was promoted to president, I was already

executive vice president. Ishida had worked with two executive vice presidents under him. Our duties were clearly divided, with Nakagawa in charge of business, and me handling the technical side of things. But with Nakagawa now president, I found, quite naturally, that business matters all converged on me. Knowing that I just couldn't handle this in addition to my other duties, I asked Ishida to appoint Shuji Ohno as executive vice president, and we returned again to the former system with me in charge of technical matters and Ohno in charge of business. Later on, I also served as executive vice president together with Shoichi Saito.

In 1962, the year after Nakagawa became president, we signed a labor-management declaration. The labor dispute of 1950 in which the company had fired a large number of workers and labor and management had clashed head-on had quieted down, but small problems continued to plague labor relations thereafter for some time. Eventually these, too, settled down and a relationship of trust gradually arose.

Mutual trust is the basis of labor relations. Labor relations at Toyota were initially marked by doubts and disbelief, but with time differences were ironed out. The labor–management declaration we signed was simply a written statement of this rapprochement. The purpose of this document was to uphold and sustain the trust that had been built up between management and labor, and to prevent backsliding by either side from this position. It also was intended as a reminder to those who came after to guard the fruits won through the sacrifices made by both sides. The spirit of this declaration still lives on at Toyota.

We also erected a marker in observance of the declaration. After all, it took about ten years for that relationship of mutual trust to take hold between labor and management.

TOYOTA AND FORD

In 1960, talk of a possible association with Ford arose for the third time, in connection with plans for producing a "national" car then being kicked around. With the Ministry of Trade and Industry strongly pushing the "national car" idea, Toyota went ahead and built a prototype of the Publica, an economy car designed for the general consumer.

But we had doubts about our ability to produce the Publica single-handed. At the same time, trade was gradually being liberalized and the possibility of opening Japan up to foreign capital was even under discussion. If Japan were thrown open to foreign investment, we had visions of Detroit and the Big Three swooping right into the Japanese market. To brake what we feared would be a disastrous influx of foreign capital and to inject some new technology from abroad, Toyota presented Ford with a proposal for jointly building a plant in Japan and there jointly manufacturing Publica cars.

The proposal called for Toyota and Ford each to contribute 40 percent of the starting capital, with the remaining 20 percent to be put up by Toyota Motor Sales. Kamiya, then president of Toyota Motor Sales, and Nakagawa, still executive vice president of Toyota, took part in the negotiations, which were held primarily in Japan.

Although I had nothing directly to do with these talks, I was asked repeatedly to guide Ford engineers on tours of our plants. The purpose of the visits was to determine whether the Publica was indeed a full-fledged car worthy of Ford's consideration. These engineers included John McDougall, who retired about five years ago as an executive vice president of Ford. The repeated visits indicated to us that, although we were saying we had developed a car for the general consumer, Ford was unwilling to take us at our word.

Talks continued for about a year, until mid-1961, but for some reason that was never made clear, the proposal was scrapped summarily by Ford at a board-of-directors meeting. Ishida was furious. "Doesn't Ford have any sense of propriety?" he fumed. True, we were the ones who had proposed the joint venture in the first place, but Ford's method of turning us down left a lot to be desired. After putting on every appearance of intending to go through with the partnership and asking for all sorts of information from Toyota, this abrupt dismissal of the matter smacked of blatant disrespect.

This was not our last attempt to form ties with Ford, however. Twenty years later, in 1980, talk again arose of building a plant together, this time in the U.S. As before, Toyota did the proposing, but the nature of the proposal was different. In 1960, we had asked Ford to teach us everything they could about small cars, but in 1980 the situation had changed. This time, we were offering to jointly produce our vehicle at Ford. The student had traded places with the teacher. This only goes to show how much the world can change in the short space of twenty years.

We attempted to form ties with Ford on a total of four occasions before and after the war, and in each case nothing came of our efforts. I suppose that we were never meant to become partners.

THE AUTO INDUSTRY REGROUPS

As the liberalization of foreign capital in Japan grew more imminent, the time became ripe for a reorganization of the domestic auto industry. The first proposal made to us was a merger with Prince Motors. This was brought up by Shojiro Ishibashi, founder and former chairman of Bridgestone, in 1964, the year of the Tokyo Olympics. Being the industrialist that he was, Ishibashi urged us from the start to take over Prince. Back then, mergers were regarded as the modus operandi for restructuring an industry.

We turned down the offer. Ishibashi had made it clear that "if things don't work out with Toyota, we'll have to go elsewhere." So we foresaw, more or less, that Nissan would take over Prince if we didn't. And that's exactly what happened.

Nissan and Prince merged in August 1966. Two months later we formed business ties with Hino Motors. Hino at the time was producing a small passenger car called the Contessa using technology from Renault, but the car wasn't selling. If a car doesn't sell, the most sensible thing to do is to stop making it, but that would have left Hino with nothing to do. And the alternative of continuing production promised to plunge the company into a rapidly spiraling debt. Whichever way it decided, Hino was in a bind.

Their main bank was the same as Toyota's—Mitsui Bank. Whenever Ishida went to Tokyo on business, he generally stopped by Mitsui. The bank was concerned about how Hino would make out, but because it lacked the confidence to rebuild the company, all it did was continue to pour capital indiscriminately into Hino in the hope that things would work out somehow. That's when Mitsui brought up with Ishida the idea of a partnership.

Negotiations initiated through Mitsui were begun on a friendly, cooperative note, but one day, Masanobu Matsukata, then president of Hino, laid a bombshell before us.

"Look," he said, "we'll stop making the Contessa, but give us something comparable to do in its place."

I could hardly believe what I had heard. The president of Hino was telling us, in no uncertain terms: "We're going to stop making cars."

That must have been an extremely hard decision for Matsukata to make. The only reason he had been able to make it was that Shoji Okubo, the former chairman of Hino who had started producing the Contessa with technical cooperation from Renault, had died of acute bronchitis in January 1965, the year we began our negotiations with Hino. Had Okubo still been alive, Matsukata probably would have found it next to impossible to say "We're going to stop making the Contessa." After all, Okubo had been decorated by the French government with the Légion d'honneur for having begun domestic production of the Renault 4CV.

Matsukata seemed to be prepared to go as far as a merger.

However, seeing that a merger would not have been in Toyota's interest and probably would have run afoul of the Antimonopoly Law, we proposed a partnership instead.

When Nissan and Prince merged, the Fair Trade Commission gave its official sanction, citing as justification that "the Nissan–Prince merger results in a market share smaller than that of Toyota." What this meant was that, as the top automaker, Toyota was not free to merge with anyone.

Yet, at the same time, MITI was vociferous in its demands for a restructuring of the industry. We decided that the Fair Trade Commission would be more likely to approve a cooperative alliance between Toyota and Hino Motors than a merger.

Matsukata scrapped Hino's pride as a passenger car maker, reneged on their obligations to Renault, and grabbed for the alliance with Toyota. This saved his company, but we had to do something about Hino's franchised dealers. Hino had two sales networks, one for their large trucks and the other for passenger cars. Once production of the Contessa was suspended, the car dealers would have nothing to sell. Even if Hino survived on production work contracted out by Toyota, its dealers would be left out in the cold.

But we weren't about to simply absorb all of Hino's dealerships into our franchises. This would have made no sense at all in cases where Toyota and Hino outlets were practically across the street from each other, as in Kyoto. We sold the Hino outlet in Kyoto and this later became a dealership for Fuji Heavy Industries. It took Hino Motors a couple of years to sell off all its Contessa dealerships.

After halting production of the Contessa, Hino made small trucks for Toyota under contract. They also later made passenger cars for us, but this was just piecework at a fixed price per unit, so it left the company's management free to concentrate on their large trucks.

At the start of our partnership with Hino, I gave Matsukata something to shoot for. "Hino's now in cahoots with the top car maker in Japan," I said. "So you've got to reach the top in trucks." And that's exactly what they did with their big trucks.

Almost immediately after we had reached an agreement with Hino Motors, Tadao Watanabe, then chairman of Sanwa Bank, approached us about working together with Daihatsu Motor.

Now, there was nothing at all wrong with Daihatsu, as a look at their balance sheet confirmed. Yet, although their profit-and-loss picture was good, that in itself didn't mean that they had a bright future ahead of them. I don't know whether it was Daihatsu president Yuji Koishi who asked Sanwa Bank to arrange for a tie-up with Toyota after judging the company's future prospects to be poor, or whether the Sanwa Bank people talked him into it themselves.

With all the talk going on about reshaping the industry, middle-rank manufacturers no longer knew where they stood. I imagine that Koishi's decision to enter into negotiations with us came only after a good deal of hesitation on his part.

As with Hino Motors, we began talks on friendly terms, but the cars made and sold by Toyota and Daihatsu were direct competitors. Toyota wasn't making mini-size vehicles (550cc and under), so we suggested that Daihatsu turn to the production of mini-size vehicles. But Koishi was less willing than Hino Motors' Matsukata had been to abandon the existing line of Daihatsu cars and was determined to go on making compacts as long as possible. That explains why Daihatsu continues even today to make standard economy cars that compete directly with Toyota, in spite of the affiliation between the two companies.

There also was talk of a tie-up with Fuji Heavy Industries, but Fuji Heavy never approached us formally on the matter. We heard indirect reports of internal disagreement within Fuji Heavy between those who wanted to form ties with Toyota and those who thought it better to ally the company with Nissan, which, like Fuji Heavy, had the support of the Industrial Bank of Japan. A personal friend of mine, Tameharu Yamada, a former senior managing director at Fuji Heavy, apparently felt an affinity for Toyota, perhaps because he himself was originally from Nagoya.

Rumors like this were constantly drifting over from Fuji Heavy, but there was never anything to grab hold of. Although we could perhaps have drawn the company over to our camp, a partnership with Fuji Heavy in addition to the agreements we had already forged with Hino and Daihatsu would have been spreading ourselves too thin. Fuji Heavy eventually set up ties with Nissan.

Although we agreed, in this domestic drama of reorganization, to undertake most of what was asked of us, we initiated no moves ourselves. This is because we were prepared to deal with any problems brought on by capital liberalization on our own terms without outside assistance. As Ishida was fond of saying, "You've got to guard your own castle by yourself."

MOTORIZATION COMES TO JAPAN

Motorization and the private ownership of cars proceeded rapidly in Japan in the years following the Tokyo Olympics. In October 1966, Toyota brought out the Corolla, which has since become a legend in its time.

While some are of the opinion that the Corolla rode the wave of motorization, I think it's the other way around. We worked to create popular demand with the Corolla and in my opinion that's just what we did. We built an engine plant (Kamigo) and an assembly plant (Takaoka) for the Corolla. It's only because we succeeded that I can afford to say so now, but had motorization not caught on in Japan, Toyota would most likely have been strapped down with surplus facilities.

In April 1966, six months before we launched the Corolla, Nissan brought out the Sunny (Sentra) with a 1000cc engine. Deciding that we'd better stay a step ahead of our arch rival, we mounted a 1100cc engine in the Corolla and stressed the appeal of that "extra 100cc" in our advertising. This strategy worked out far better than we'd anticipated.

The car was marketed late in the year, so production in 1966 came to only 12,000 units. In 1967, however, we made 160,000 Corollas, and from then on up through 1972, yearly production rose steadily in annual jumps of 100,000 units. The car went through several model changes, with cumulative production reaching five million units in June 1976 and ten million units in March 1983. In 1980, the single best year we had for this line, Toyota made 856,000 Corollas.

The name Corolla has become familiar to people the world over, but it doesn't sound the same everywhere. In Japan, it's pronounced "carora," which rhymes with "aurora" because the consonants r and l can't be distinguished in Japanese. And in Puerto Rico, people pronounce it "coroya."

Corolla is a Latin-derived term meaning essentially "crown of the flower." We gave all our early passenger cars names associated with "crown" because our first passenger car, the Crown, had been something of a success and this was a good image we wanted to keep. Thus Corona, for example, literally means "crown of the sun."

Deciding on the name of a car is a very real struggle in which the "feel" of the word and many other factors come into play. When we were looking for a name for the Corolla, I collected a list of possibilities from which a decision was made without too much trouble. Usually, however, reaching a consensus on a name is almost impossible. Often the people in charge of this will run out of time and bring the matter directly to me. Once, when we ran out of ideas, we borrowed the Japanese word for crown: kanmuri. That's how we came up with Camry. Naming a car is something like naming one's children. One thing that is clear, though, is that no matter how good the name is, if the product itself is no good, it just won't sell.

Motorization continued at a pace that had even us surprised. When we were preparing to launch the Corolla, I thought that someday there'd be one car for every five people in Japan. With a population of one hundred million, this adds up to twenty million cars. Assuming that car owners traded in their cars once every ten years, I figured that this would translate into a demand of two million new cars a year. I reckoned that as long as we didn't produce more than two million cars a year, we wouldn't have to worry about oversupply, but our estimates turned out to be very, very conservative.

Today, overall annual production in Japan has surged past the ten million mark, and the number of cars owned and operated in Japan is now forty-four million. That comes to one car for every 2.7 people. This in itself is a good indicator of how much the Japanese economy has grown.

PRESIDENT OF TOYOTA

Nakagawa passed away suddenly on October 13, 1967, only a year after we had launched the Corolla. Two weeks later, on October 30, I was appointed president.

I felt no different as president than I had as a managing director or executive vice president. What amazed me, however, was the difference in attitude of those around me. Everyone began treating me as The President. People tend to see the president of a company as being much more exalted, of greater stature, than the vice president. Now they were looking at me that way.

Someone who joins a large company at the bottom of the ladder and works his way to the top may have a special sense of elation on making it to the presidency, but I had entered a small company called Toyoda Automatic Loom Works that was started and run by relatives. When Toyota was founded, aside from Kiichiro, only I and Shoichi Saito had graduated from college. Unless we stood up and took the initiative ourselves, the company wasn't going to go anywhere. We had to stay on our toes. Then, before I knew it, the company had grown into a large corporation and I was sitting at the top.

At the first press conference I held after becoming president, reporters asked me: "Did your appointment have anything to do with your being a member of the Toyoda family?" The question took me completely by surprise.

"I believe that I was chosen because I'm suitable for the job," I responded. That line caught a lot of attention in the media and became famous for a while.

Almost by definition, the possibility always exists of the vice president of a company taking over someday for the president. When Ishida retired to become chairman, Nakagawa, who was then senior executive vice president, rose to the post of president. Later, when Nakagawa died suddenly, it was only natural that I be appointed as the next president. That's all there was to it.

The newspapers next day were plastered with headlines proclaiming: POWER RETURNS TO THE TOYODA CLAN. That's when I realized just how sensational and misleading the papers and mass media can be.

It's true that when Toyota was founded, the Toyoda family controlled the company; but after the war, company stock was offered up for public subscription. By the time I was appointed president, I doubt that anyone still thought of Toyota as belonging to the Toyoda family.

In February 1967, the year that I became president, cumulative sales of Toyoda cars, trucks, and buses reached the three million mark. A few years after that, the company turned out more vehicles than it had produced cumulatively while Risaburo, Kiichiro, Ishida, and Nakagawa were president. Then, in 1980, Toyota achieved an annual production level of more than three million units.

On November 16, about one month after Nakagawa died, I was appointed a vice president of the Japan Automobile Manufacturers Association (JAMA). JAMA had been formed in April of that year as an organization of domestic automakers by consolidating the Automobile Manufacturers Association and the Japan Small Automobile Manufacturers Association. The first president of JAMA was Katsuji Kawamata, president of Nissan.

There were three vice presidents: Nakagawa, Yuji Koishi of Daihatsu, and Soichiro Honda of Honda Motor. With Nakagawa's death, I automatically became a vice president at the executive committee meeting held the following month.

AUTO EMISSION CONTROLS: FINDING THE ANSWER

I was president of Toyota for fifteen years, from 1967 to 1982, a period which, if I had to characterize it succinctly, I'd call "smooth sailing." The most trying episodes in those years were the two oil crises and the controversy over auto emissions regulations.

Controlling auto emissions first arose as an issue in the early 1960s with a campaign in the U.S. to regulate emissions. But the real difficulties date back to when U.S. Senator Muskie started pushing for legal controls in the States. The Muskie Bill became law in December 1970. Half a year later, in July 1971, the Environment Agency was established in Japan. In September that same year, the new agency drafted a long-term emissions control plan and presented it to the Central Council for Control of Environmental Pollution for study. The following year, the council submitted its report to the agency in which it laid out recommendations for auto emissions standards to be met by 1975 and 1976.

In 1970, when the lead pollution problem cropped up at Yanagicho in Shinjuku, Tokyo, and a great hue and cry arose over photochemical smog, it was hard to tell whether regulations were really necessary or not. Our Hanji Umehara once said: "If the air is that bad at the Yanagi-cho intersection, they should put up a big fan and blast it out of there." What he meant was to blow the exhaust gases off with a fan when the pollutant concentrations at a given spot got too high. Once the exhaust thins, the parts per million will come down. Installing a few fans rather than regulating all cars would certainly seem to be a more effective way of dealing with the local buildup of emissions.

Umehara didn't keep his comments confined to the company,

so the press started getting on our case, accusing the company of "talking nonsense." Umehara was actually saying that such an alternative would be less expensive than regulating automobile emissions, but the point of his argument seems to have been lost on the press.

Although cars were not the sole source of exhaust gases, because the Clean Air Act had been enacted in the U.S., short of stopping exports to America, there was no way for us to circumvent the problem.

I was once asked by the chairman of Renault, after the Clean Air Act had been passed: "So what do you think of America's emissions regulations?"

"They're a disaster," I replied.

Instead of simply agreeing with me, he blurted out: "I refuse to pay any attention to a country that does such idiotic things. Renault is going to stop exports to the U.S."

The problem was solved instantly for those willing to cut off exports to the U.S., but that just was not an option open to Japanese automakers.

In Japan, as the problem of emissions took on increasing proportions, changing from a local issue to a question of the public's health, we came to realize that Toyota, too, would have no choice but to confront the issue head-on. The only question that remained was whether Japan needed to adopt wholesale the same regulations as those contained in the Clean Air Act. For a while we held our ground, telling the Environment Agency: "If these regulations are necessary, show us the proof."

Naturally, we knew that there was little solid evidence to support the case for tighter regulations. The only answer the Agency could give us was: "It's better to have clean air than dirty air."

"But implementing auto emissions controls will raise the price of cars," we insisted.

"Money is of no concern when it comes to people's health," they replied. "You can't buy health with money."

There was nothing we could say to that.

We now had a big problem on our hands. How would we carry out emissions controls? To begin with, we needed time for preparations. The controls were to be made stricter by degrees. As in the high jump, the bar would be set low at first, then gradually raised. Emissions standards for the most difficult pollutants, oxides of nitrogen from passenger cars, were to begin at 2.18 grams per kilometer and eventually be cut almost tenfold to a final value of 0.25 gram. Clearing the initial value would be relatively easy, but as a manufacturer we had to think about clearing that final bar setting of 0.25 gram right from the very start.

It would do no good to satisfy emissions control standards if this meant making concessions in engine performance. Taking a more extreme view of the matter, if no one drove cars, there'd be no emissions to worry about and we'd all be assured of clean air to breathe. But then we wouldn't be talking about cars anymore. So we had to find a way of both maintaining our existing performance levels and meeting the standards. That was the minimum goal that Toyota set for itself. We saw little hope of meeting the final target of 0.25 gram NO_x by the date specified, so we asked for an extension. However, the Environment Agency rode roughshod over the auto industry. The controls were given precedence, so the cars built to meet the initial standards were gas guzzlers that ran poorly and had no power.

The most unpleasant ordeal I had to go through during this entire controversy over emissions was being called in to testify in hearings at the National Diet, fed all sorts of dubious arguments, then having the press lash out with comments like: "Cut the grousing and just clean up the air." The whole thing was like a witchhunt. People who didn't know the first thing about emissions were making a lot of fuss, and all this was accepted as perfectly proper. It was a very bitter experience for me. The Diet members and newspaper reporters asking the questions were all laymen. Calling auto emissions dirty is one thing, but it isn't something you can see with your own eyes.

Technically speaking, cleaning up emissions is a very difficult problem. Yet, when we tried to explain things in the simplest possible terms, we were told: "There's no time for that." Even those who listened carefully to our explanations would back off as soon as the discussion got a bit involved, saying: "I'm no specialist." Then at the end they'd say: "So all you have to do is clean up the air." Why, at that rate, we couldn't even have a decent argument.

The nine domestic automakers were summoned to the Environment Agency in May 1973 for a public hearing on the auto emissions problem. The director of the agency was Takeo Miki, who later became prime minister. Miki and I argued back and forth quite a bit over this issue.

By this time I had become chairman of the Japan Automobile Manufacturers Association, so I had to address myself to the debate over emissions both as president of Toyota and chairman of the JAMA. My duty as chairman was to make certain that the agency set up regulations which could be met by all the manufacturers. Thus, if one automaker raised its hand to say, "We can do it," but the other eight companies said they couldn't, as chairman this left me in a fix. But it's difficult to learn anything about other companies. Whenever I'd ask: "What's the situation over at your company?" I never got a straight answer. Under the circumstances, I found that the easiest way to present a unified front was to flex Toyota's muscle as the top domestic maker by saying that we couldn't meet the standards.

This drew a great deal of fire from the press, who lit into us with allegations and innuendo: "Something's wrong if Honda and Mazda claim they can do it but Toyota, the leading maker, says it can't." That's when I learned to take the punishment the papers dish out.

One difficulty with the emissions standards that Toyota alone faced was tied in with the large number of models we made. Even if we were able to meet the standards without a loss of performance in one model, this didn't necessarily mean that we would be able to do the same in our other models. That's why it was entirely possible that a company making just one or two models might be able to reduce its emissions to the designated levels while Toyota could not.

Since emissions controls were something entirely new to us, what worked in the Crown might not be effective in the Corolla. Developing a different strategy for each car would take a long time. We had the whole company working on the problem, but when we learned of the merits of the low-emissions CVCC (compound vortex-controlled combustion) engine developed by Honda, we swallowed our pride and asked them for the technology. These efforts were applauded by the Environment Agency, and so we were able to have the enforcement date for the 1976 standards moved back another two years.

This extension enabled us to meet the standards in all of our models, but I still think that those regulations were a brutal way to get the job done. It was like teaching someone how to swim by throwing him into the water and having him thrash about for his very life. One mistake and it would be all over. However, those controls did help us make large gains on Western automotive technology.

From the very start, Toyota had considered using catalysts as a means of cleaning up engine emissions without lowering performance, so we learned everything we could about the use of catalysts. Catalysts, which accelerate or promote the combination of one substance with another, are used primarily in the chemical industry, where they are employed under the best possible conditions. The proper way to use a catalyst is under the temperature and pressure conditions that allow it to work most effectively.

In motor vehicles, however, the catalyst must be adapted to the operating conditions of the vehicle. Depending on where it runs, the temperature in a car may rise or fall. The car itself rattles and shakes. But the catalyst must go on working regardless of the conditions under which the car is driven. The demands placed on such catalysts differ entirely from catalysts used in the chemical industry.

The question we needed to answer was what type of catalyst to use. We met the 1975 and 1976 standards with oxidation catalysts, but these wouldn't suffice for the more stringent 1978 standards, on which we had received a two-year extension. We wanted to avoid using platinum if at all possible because of its great expense, so we searched everywhere for suitable alternatives, all to no avail.

Meanwhile, the deadline was approaching. With time running out on us, we decided to go with the noble metals platinum and rhodium, and even searched abroad for a platinum mine to supply us with the needed ore. We also were approached by owners of platinum mines who offered to open up new mines and supply us with the ore if we agreed to a long-term purchasing arrangement. Even today, the auto industry continues to be a large user of platinum.

More than ten years have passed since the emissions standards were first enforced, and rapid progress has been made in auto emissions control technology. In May 1984, Toyota brought out a new Carina with a front-mounted engine and front-wheel drive that uses an oxidation catalyst rather than a three-way catalyst to cut auto emissions. We used electronic technology to develop a new engine with a lean combustion control system. This drastically cut the generation of emissions by the engine, enabling us to meet existing standards with just an oxidation catalyst. What's so special about the new engine is that it assures the stable combustion of even lean mixtures, resulting in a big improvement in fuel economy over the use of three-way catalysts.

THE ROTARY ENGINE TALKS

We began negotiations in the early 1970s with Toyo Kogyo—renamed Mazda Motor in 1984—for the supplying of Wankel rotary engines to Toyota. This had nothing whatsoever to do with the regrouping of the auto industry a few years earlier.

In 1971, Toyota had bought up the patent rights from West Germany's Audi NSU and Wankel and begun development research on the engine, but before long we learned that full development of the Wankel was impossible with just the basic patents. Mazda held all the peripheral patents. Without access to these, there was no way we could develop the engine for commercial use. That's when we decided to enter into negotiations with Mazda.

The initial aim of our talks with Mazda was the licensing of their patents, but this led to discussions on the purchase by Toyota of fully built rotary engines. Negotiations dragged on for months. Then, while this was going on, the first oil crisis hit. Since the rotary had a low fuel economy, we abandoned our plans to develop it and brought the talks to an end.

Our interest in the Wankel engine had stemmed from the fact that it could deliver high performance in ways unlike the piston engine. We didn't think that the piston engine would be entirely replaced by the Wankel, but given that General Motors had also begun research on this engine, just to be on the safe side we had decided to set up a program of our own. No one could afford to ignore what GM was up to. If the world's largest automaker was investing big bucks in the development of the rotary engine, then there was every possibility that this would someday become the wave of the future.

GM had actually built a special plant tooled for production of the Wankel. But, like Toyota, when the oil crisis broke, the company scrapped its production plans. Edward Cole, president of GM at the time, took the blame for it and quit. To compound one misfortune with another, he died shortly after that in an airplane crash. Toyota didn't get involved with the Wankel as deeply as did GM, so I wasn't placed in Cole's position of having to resign.

Mazda suffered the consequences of the fuel crises even more than GM. Kohei Matsuda, president of Mazda at the time, seems to have staked the future of his company on the Wankel.

Although this was effective in holding down pollutant emissions, compared to the piston engine its fuel economy left too much to be desired. Despite the excitement this engine generated in the early 1970s, then, it never stood a chance of dominating the auto industry.

I'll readily admit, though, that the Wankel has features all of its own. Kohei Matsuda's efforts at developing it for commercial production are highly significant because they moved forward the state of the art. That in itself deserves merit.

THE OIL SHOCKS

The first oil crisis came in October 1973, at a time when we were still preoccupied with the emissions control regulations. There had been strange, ominous rumblings since the beginning of the year, however. Japan was at the high-water mark of its postwar affluence: we had a superheated economy and consumer purchasing power had grown enormously. The auto business was a seller's market. Those of us in the business continued making cars because they were selling as fast as we could turn them out. This state of affairs persisted for quite some time.

Yet, at the same time, there had been a succession of major accidents at chemical plants. One incident that had a direct effect on Toyota was an explosion at a chemical plant in Yamaguchi Prefecture. The plant caught fire and production came to a standstill. When the Sanyo railway line closed down as a result and raw materials for tire production ran low, we made cars without spare tires for a short while. The economy was so hot back then that even these sold.

The plants were running at full capacity and we were short of labor, so we asked our dealers to send over people to lend us a hand. However, starting in early summer, materials became increasingly hard to get hold of. This situation continued to worsen until the plant explosion in Yamaguchi. Then, in the fall, materials suddenly became very scarce.

The fourth Middle East war had flared up just before this, on

October 6, precipitating the oil crisis. Shortly after this conflict, a leading politician created quite a stir when, asked how long a supply of petroleum Japan had on hand, he replied: "Just two weeks' worth." The hostilities in the Mideast soon quieted down, but it wasn't until early the following year that the effects of the oil crisis became fully apparent.

Somehow or other, we managed to scrape together enough materials to maintain full production through the end of 1973, but the following year we immediately began to cut back on our output. Sales had come tumbling down partly as a result of our two recent price hikes, one in December 1973 and the other at the start of 1974. The sluggish sales had driven up dealer inventories, so we steadily lowered production starting shortly after New Year's and continuing through March.

Just as Toyota was beginning to trim its production, some of the other domestic automakers were giving the go-ahead for big production increases. I believe we were the first to cut back on our output. We completed inventory adjustments with our dealers in March and again raised production the following month. The situation didn't turn out as bad as we had feared, in part because we'd been able to cut production so quickly.

Priority for increased production went to the Corolla. Domestic sales hit a peak in 1973 and declined somewhat in 1974. Yet the Corolla was selling well. We also were concentrating more on our exports, which continued to rise rapidly from 1974 to 1975.

In 1975, we had to contend with both the problem of auto emissions and the second oil shock, a combination that was almost overwhelming. I was no longer able to devote all of my energies to company work. In fact, so much of my time was taken up with my duties as president of JAMA that I was able to spend only about a quarter of my time on company matters. Masaya Hanai, former chairman of Toyota Motor Company, became my right-hand man and ran affairs within the company for me during this trying period.

I was appointed president of JAMA in May 1972 and continued

to serve in that capacity for four terms, until 1980. When I assumed the presidency, the problems of product recalls and of liberalizing foreign capital investment in Japan had been more or less resolved. Nissan's Kawamata, who had been president since 1967, one day dropped by my office and told me: "I'm going to quit as president. Why don't you take over for me?" I had no special objections, so, without thinking much about it, I accepted.

Before being appointed, I had thought: "This shouldn't take too much of my time." That wasn't to be the case. Time after time, I was summoned to the Diet to give testimony on the problem of auto emissions. I also took part in the conference between JAMA and the Society of Motor Manufacturers and Traders of England, and was called upon to attend countless other functions and events.

If the presidency itself had been my only duty, then this wouldn't have taken up so much of my time; but an almost endless list of posts go along with the position, including membership on MITI's Industrial Structure Council. What's more, most of the meetings for these posts were set on fixed days, forcing me to arrange my schedule around them. It takes two hours to get from Nagoya to Tokyo by bullet train and another hour to reach Nagoya from our headquarters. In other words, I had to travel a total of six hours to attend a two-hour meeting, so a single meeting in Tokyo took a whole day out of my schedule.

Government councils are usually dormant when there are no problems or issues to stir the air. However, if something does come up, they roar into action. During the period that I served on the Industrial Structure Council, one problem after another cropped up, from emissions standards to the restructuring of industries, so I was constantly receiving notices of upcoming meetings. It didn't matter whether I had other plans or not: I was always expected to attend. In 1980, I handed over the JAMA presidency to Nissan's Takashi Ishihara.

The Toyota Foundation

We established the Toyota Foundation in October 1974. The years 1972 and 1973 had brought Japan to the pinnacle of its postwar prosperity, and loud cries now went up calling upon corporations to assume greater "social responsibility." Toyota, like many other successful companies, was repeatedly lambasted for being "too profitable."

Even though we were branded overly profitable, we had to make enormous capital investments for our safety and antipollution programs, and we also needed to revamp and reinforce the company radically to prepare for the international showdown we knew was coming in the auto industry. In fact, it was only because of the buffering effect of the profits we had accumulated internally during the rapid-growth era of motorization in the late 1960s and early 1970s that we were able to cut back so dramatically on production during the oil crisis.

Yet it is not always possible to present the company's case up front. We therefore decided, in 1973, to set up a private foundation as one part of our contribution to society.

Preparations immediately got under way, but I soon realized that neither I nor anyone else at Toyota knew very much about private foundations. It was apparent to us that, whatever type of foundation we did set up, selecting the right person to head it was the quickest approach we could take. We looked at many different candidates and ultimately settled on Yujiro Hayashi, who had been the director of the Economic Research Institute at the Economic Planning Agency and was at the time a professor at the Tokyo Institute of Technology. After being persuaded by Shotaro Kamiya, then president of Toyota Motor Sales, and me, Hayashi agreed to become executive director of the foundation.

In spite of the attention we gave to this project, establishment of the Toyota Foundation took close to a year, mainly because we tried to give the foundation a broad charter. In Japan, private foundations are placed under the supervision of one government agency or another. Depending on the purpose and goals of our foundation, it might be assigned to the Ministry of Education, the Ministry of Trade and Industry, or even the Ministry of Transport. However, if the foundation fell under the control of any specific government agency, its activities would be restricted. What I had in mind was an organization with a broad sphere of activity, so I decided to place the foundation under the jurisdiction of the Prime Minister's Office and went to ask for their cooperation.

Officials at the office told me: "We've never overseen such a large foundation." But they went ahead and studied the idea anyway. When everything was settled, the Toyota Foundation was established as the first large, multipurpose foundation under the jurisdiction of the Prime Minister's Office, with me as chairman.

The foundation was set up to promote research, for which it was given an initial endowment of three billion yen. This was Hayashi's idea, and I fully supported it. I left the actual administration of the foundation entirely in his hands, taking the liberty only of clarifying the fundamental purpose underlying its existence. In brief, this was as follows. If the research concerned a business activity that was reasonably profitable, then industrialists put up the money. If it related to an area that didn't lend itself directly to profit-making, but showed promise as basic research, then funds would be made available to universities conducting such research. Our reasoning was that, if you drill where there's thought to be oil, there will always be people willing and eager to put up the costs. But no one wants to back a drilling effort where there may be no oil. That's where the foundation comes in. Naturally, whether the research paid off in returns to Toyota or not was never a concern of ours.

The Toyota Foundation celebrated the tenth anniversary of its founding in 1984. By then, the endowment had grown to eleven billion yen, making it one of a select group of large private foundations in Japan. Grants are provided by the foundation for research both in Japan and abroad. At the moment, most of the overseas grant activity is concentrated in Southeast Asia, but eventually we want to extend this throughout the entire world.

The Toyota Foundation does more than just dispense aid. It also works in association with leading American foundations. Up until 1983, for instance, it provided scholarship grants to Japanese students studying abroad in a joint program with the Ford Foundation. (Each of the two foundations supplied half of the scholarship funds.) The foundation also has taken over programs established by other foundations, such as the research program on traditional architecture begun in Southeast Asia with funds supplied by the Rockefeller Foundation. We intend to continue increasing the Toyota Foundation's activities in a broad range of areas.

THE TOYOTA TECHNOLOGICAL INSTITUTE

While the Toyota Foundation serves the important function of funding and promoting research, the Toyota Technological Institute (TTI) was opened in April 1981 with a broader mission: to train and educate young developmental engineers and scientists for service to the nation.

At Toyota, as at any corporation, there are a significant number of individuals who, although they had the desire and ability, did not attend college. What could we do to help these people go to school? One possibility was to have a company give such employees scholarships and place them on temporary leave for the duration of their studies. But since university education today leans disproportionately toward academics, we felt that this would offer little opportunity for the training and character-building that Toyota had in mind.

The only way I saw of supporting young adults burning with a desire to learn and educating them as responsible, well-rounded individuals was for Toyota to open up its own institute of higher learning. Taking the long view of things, we were convinced that setting up a university along the lines we had in mind to educate students who would return to their respective companies once they had completed their studies, there to make valuable contributions, could only serve the national interest. And each company would gain by being able to hold on to its gifted employees.

Since total character development was one of our primary goals, we felt that, rather than attending lectures in cramped classrooms and doing research with the limited facilities and equipment that a university had to offer, research conducted on real problems in real factories after acquiring a thorough grounding in the basics through university study constituted a far more valuable learning experience. As much as possible, we wanted to offer the students individualized learning on a one-to-one basis with professors, so we also felt it best to have all the students live in dormitories for at least part of the four years. And because the students would be fully housed in dormitories, enrollment had to be limited.

Having thus formulated our plans for a school, we petitioned the Ministry of Education for permission to establish it. But the ministry wasn't easily won over. While ministry officials professed to agree with the "spirit" of our plans, they just wouldn't grant us permission to go ahead. Even the ministry, powerful as it is, wasn't about to show open resistance to our intentions, but I wonder if perhaps the officials there didn't feel that we were rejecting the educational policy that the ministry had pursued since the end of the war.

The biggest reason behind the Ministry of Education's reluctance to grant us permission for the school was the existence of a law which said, in effect, that no new universities and colleges would be built in Tokyo, Osaka, Nagoya, and other cities designated by government decree. Setting up the school in Toyota City would present no special problem, but since practical factory training at various companies was to be among the formal courses of instruction offered, the school should not be located at too great a distance from the plants of the companies concerned.

Our search for an appropriate site ended with the decision to locate it in Nagoya on the site vacated by the Toyota Central Research & Development Laboratories. Building the school there would allow it to make full use of the research center's old facilities. After repeated explanations to the Ministry of Education of our true intentions in founding the school, we finally received formal approval.

Naturally, it takes good teachers to train good students. Good teachers not only had to be academically qualified, they also had to endorse the thinking and philosophy behind the institute and be willing to pour energy and enthusiasm into their work. We had to gather together a teaching staff with the zeal it took to live with the students in the dormitories and teach.

I asked Kyoto University professor Fujio Nagao, who we had informally selected as the first president of TTI, to set up a recruiting center. This then became the nucleus of our efforts to recruit good teachers from all over the country. We were fortunate in having quite a few outstanding teachers come to us from national and private universities as well as the industrial community.

Some of the professors at the institute expressed doubts as to whether individuals who had joined a corporation and worked there for a couple of years could become good students and profit fully from their studies. The Ministry of Education came at us as well with the suggestion that we consider also accepting graduates fresh out of high school rather than just people who had experience working in industry. But we explained to the ministry that such students would not be in keeping with the intent and spirit behind the founding of the school.

TTI graduated its first class of students in spring 1985. Looking back on these four years, I can say with complete confidence that the doubts held by some of the teachers were entirely unfounded and that our selection of students was definitely not mistaken. These first graduates have now returned to their former companies. Whether those companies feel that the institute has done a good job in educating their employees is something we will have to learn over time.

The institute accepts a maximum of 80 students per class and offers two basic curricula. Since there was no need to go out of our way to fill the school to capacity, the first year we accepted only 38 students out of the 226 who applied. To be eligible to enroll in Toyota Technological Institute, a student must first be employed by some company. Perhaps then, in the future, if individuals begin joining companies in order to gain entry to the school, we will be certain to get students of even higher caliber.

Another concern that had been on the minds of the professors at the school was the factory training portion of the curriculum. The idea was to ask various companies to accept working interns from the institute and train them for a given period of time in their respective plants with the latest tools and equipment. But if for some reason companies were unwilling to open their doors to our students, our efforts and intentions in establishing the school would have all been for naught. It was our good fortune, however, that several companies in the Nagoya region alone agreed to take on the students as trainees.

The institute set up a graduate school in 1984. At first, the Ministry of Education refused to listen to our "outrageous" proposal. "A graduate school is a place of learning for students with undergraduate degrees," we were told. "Never before has a college created a graduate school before even graduating a single undergraduate student."

What the ministry said made perfect sense. Only, we saw things a little differently. Our thinking on the matter ran as follows. Most of the students enrolled at TTI are on leave from their home companies. Some are even drawing a salary while they study. Graduating students who plan to continue their studies at the graduate school will have to extend their leave of absence a minimum of two years. This comes to a total of six years. Just how willing would a company be to welcome someone back who has been away from the job for six years? That's why we felt that there would be few instances in which graduates of the institute would go on immediately to the graduate school.

We reasoned instead that it would be more meaningful to select and educate individuals who had graduated from another college and entered a company somewhere and who now wanted to continue their studies. Moreover, the companies at which they worked would be more willing to release their employees for the two years required for such studies. Of course, students who had taken their undergraduate studies at the institute and returned for a while to their home companies also would be welcome. We basically thought of the undergraduate division and the graduate division as separate and distinct. This explained why we had thought of setting up the graduate program even before the institute had graduated any students from its undergraduate division, and had gone to the Ministry of Education for permission.

We persisted and in the end prevailed; the ministry eventually came around to our view and approved the establishment of the graduate school.

In spring 1984, the graduate school administered entrance exams to applicants recommended by their companies. Twenty-five students were accepted for the first class, although the limit was officially 24. We recruited students again in 1985 and this time accepted 26. As we had expected, only 2 students entered the graduate school directly from the undergraduate program.

The Toyota Central Research & Development Laboratories

More than anything else, the real wellspring of corporate growth and development is technology. There was a time, not so long ago, when Japanese corporations borrowed technology from abroad. But in this "high-tech" age of rapid scientific and engineering reform, to survive, a company has to have its own facilities for developing new technology.

The Toyota Group, after all, was begun by Sakichi Toyoda,

one of Japan's foremost inventors. Each company in the group specifically states, in its articles of incorporation, that it shall conduct "research for the purpose of invention." That's the spirit that prompted nine companies in the group—Toyota Motor Corporation, Toyoda Automatic Loom Works, Nippondenso, Aishin Seiki, Toyota Auto Body, Aichi Steel Works, Toyoda Spinning & Weaving, Toyoda Machine Works, and Toyota Tsusho Corporation—to establish the Toyota Central Research & Development Laboratories (TCRDL) in 1960.

The Toyota Group has inherited Sakichi's thinking. One mission of the group is to discover and invent new things, and to turn these innovations into new business. But when pressed by the constant demands of routine work, there is never time for research. The only solution is a facility for basic research removed from the hustle and bustle of normal company work. That was the purpose behind the founding of this research center.

Although TCRDL was set up with lofty goals, the reasons behind its establishment were largely pragmatic. Companies in the group were all short of funds. It made more sense to pool the resources of the individual companies than to have each doing isolated research. Participation in the facility was not limited to companies within the Toyota Group, but open also to outside suppliers.

Suppose, for example, that someone at Toyota wanted to do an analysis on a rolled steel product but none of our suppliers or affiliates had the necessary equipment. His only choice would be to have a machine-testing laboratory in Nagoya do the analysis for him. With a central R&D facility capable of handling such tests, there'd be someone available to do this right away, and the results would become the common property of the group.

Although we had grand visions for the research center, we started the facility in the early 1960s on a very practical footing by attending to our immediate research needs. Later, with the spread of motorization throughout Japan and the resulting growth enjoyed by companies in the Toyota Group, it became possible at last to rise to the challenge of our original vision. We decided to double the size of the facility, but because the original site—now occupied by the Toyota Technological Institute—was too small, we moved the center to an entirely new location. Although this new site is about twice as large, the facility itself has not yet doubled in size. Yet it is well on the way. And we have every intention of expanding it further. Close to 60,000 people work at Toyota, and more than 150,000 work within the Toyota Group. We have a responsibility to search for new work to support these people while we continue to remain profitable.

The facility really came through for us when we had to deal with the problem of emissions controls. Toyota used catalysts to control auto emissions, but when this issue first arose we didn't have a single specialist on catalysts. There were, however, a number of catalyst people at TCRDL, and they're the ones who led our successful effort to study and use catalysts for controlling emissions. We had no right, in principle, to ask the facility for help on the emissions problem or anything else, as this was counter to the purpose for which the facility was established. However, a manufacturer of machine goods like Toyota knows nothing about chemistry. So we went to TCRDL for help. That experience gave us a deeper appreciation of the importance of basic research, which is why we decided to double the size of the facility.

I think that the future will provide the laboratories with an opportunity to make full use of their enormous potential. A unique feature of the facility is its status as a joint-stock company. There don't seem to be very many research institutes set up in this way. When Nomura Securities founded the Nomura Research Institute in 1965, the people at Nomura came over and asked us a lot of questions.

THE INSTITUTE FOR INTERNATIONAL ECONOMIC STUDIES

When we set up TCRDL to pursue technical development in 1960, we discussed whether we shouldn't also have a center dedicated to the study of economic and social topics—a sort of think tank, if you will. But for a long time we were too preoccupied with hard-core technological development to give this much serious consideration, so we tabled the idea. With the merger of Toyota Motor and Toyota Motor Sales in July 1982, however, we took another look at the future of the new Toyota Motor Corporation and came to the conclusion that the need had arrived for a cultural research organization.

Technical research institutes such as TCRDL require both people and facilities, but a cultural research institute depends entirely on the people who run the place. It's the same as a foundation. I discussed the idea with the late Nobuhiko Ushiba, former minister of state for external economic affairs, and we decided to name it the Institute for International Economic Studies (IIES), because by now Toyota's activities had become global. Naturally, the chairman of the board had to be someone with a broad outlook and a keen insight into world affairs and the international scene. The only person around who filled the bill was Ushiba himself.

My association with Ushiba goes back well over twenty years. I was originally introduced to him by Yoshihiko Nakamura, a former managing director of Toyota Auto Body who had originally been with Toyota. Nakamura and Ushiba were classmates at Tokyo University, where they both belonged to the school boating club. When I first met him, Ushiba was working at the foreign ministry. Ever since then, we'd kept in constant touch.

It would not be an exaggeration to say that I set up IIES with Ushiba specifically in mind as the chairman. There's little doubt in my mind that had Ushiba not been willing to become chairman, the institute would never have been established. The same is true of the Toyota Foundation and the Toyota Technological Institute. The selection of a director is always critical. Bunroku Yoshino, former ambassador to West Germany, later took Ushiba's place as chairman, so I expect that the institute will become fully active before long.

Like TCRDL, IIES is organized as a joint-stock corporation that, at least in principle, operates on commissions received for research requested by third parties. This works well enough for TCRDL, which can more than adequately support itself on research for the Toyota Group. The same is not the case, however, with IIES. Nomura Research Institute (NRI) apparently had the same problem at first. Initially, with no orders coming in to NRI from outside customers, Nomura Securities intervened by routing assignments to NRI. After a while, orders began arriving from other sources and business grew until eventually NRI was able to go it alone without support from the parent company.

IIES, however, is still fully supported by Toyota. We haven't even gotten around to deciding what to do should orders come in someday from the Toyota Group or even sources outside the group, the reason being that the institute isn't yet fully staffed. Actually we haven't had the chance to give this our undivided attention, so the institute remains at a nascent stage.

Toyota Merges with Toyota

In January 1982, the directors of Toyota Motor Company (TMC) and Toyota Motor Sales Company (TMS) reached a formal decision to merge the two companies. Six months later, on July 1, the Toyota Motor Corporation was established. Shoichiro Toyoda was appointed president of the new company, and I assumed the chairmanship.

The story of this merger begins with the division of the original company into two separate companies thirty-five years ago. In spring 1950, Toyota was forcibly split into Toyota Motor and Toyota Motor Sales at the insistence of the banks in order to avert bankruptcy. By acquiescing with the banks' demands and breaking the company in two, we were able to receive help from them and get back on our feet again. For that saving support I will always feel grateful.

Still, the fact remains that, even though we were on the verge of collapse, breaking a single company with all its day-to-day routines into two separate organizations leaves a lot of lingering aftereffects. The only way to overcome these was through integrated management.

To push this idea of integrated management, shortly after the split I suggested to Shotaro Kamiya that we carry out some sort of personnel exchange. He gave his tentative approval; so, to balance off those members of the technical staff who were going to be working with Toyota Motor Sales, I drew up a list of people who had been involved in sales that we would be keeping at Toyota Motor. Kamiya's response was: "We're starting off with nothing. The least you can do is let me have those people who worked in sales before the split. Later, when we get onto a firmer footing, I'll send them back to you a few at a time."

What he said made sense. Since we agreed in principle, I was willing to wait a while before starting to trade staff. The only problem was that, when we did begin, the flow of personnel was entirely one way. TMC would send TMS some of its staff, but hardly anyone came over from TMS in return. They apparently needed all the people they could get, which is why, as time went on, none of the people we sent over ever came back.

Although the personnel exchange program never turned out as I had hoped, the two companies were able to integrate their respective operations fairly well. I'm convinced, in fact, that this is why Toyota was able to ride the wave of motorization so well in Japan.

When it came to production and sales, however, TMC and TMS did work each other over pretty fiercely. There's no denying that this left outside observers with the impression that we were always fighting. As a matter of fact, I wouldn't doubt that even within the two companies quite a few low-level managers thought the same thing. Each side had its way of seeing things. We'd come at each other, trading views and arguing back and forth, but in the end we'd invariably find a point of agreement and settle the score. We always eventually saw eye-to-eye. We were in this together, after all, and had the same goal of boosting sales of Toyota cars.

I began to give some serious thought to a merger around 1969, after I'd been appointed president of Toyota Motor. Up until about the mid-1960s, most of our sales had been on the domestic market, but exports began to pick up in the late 1960s and the number of our overseas dealers also grew. Toyota Motor Sales handled all dealer contracts. Dealers abroad often had a hard time understanding why cars made by Toyota Motor were purchased through Toyota Motor Sales. Dealers at home were familiar with the situation and knew the circumstances behind the split in 1950; those people abroad did not. Some even had their doubts about why TMS existed in the first place.

One way to quell these suspicions by our overseas dealers would have been to have TMC handle all exports and let Toyota Motor Sales devote itself exclusively to domestic sales. This was precisely what Hino Motors, with which we had business ties, was doing. Even Ford over in the United States had taken this approach at one time, although it had later unified its sales operations. But rather than taking such a troublesome approach, the surest and quickest solution for Toyota was clearly a merger. The two companies had originally been one, so a merger seemed the most natural course of action.

One day, I tactfully proposed the idea of a merger to Kamiya. "Don't you think it's about time we started thinking of bringing the companies back together again?" I asked. But the thought of a merger hadn't entered his mind. I had popped the question to him all of a sudden, so of course he wasn't prepared to give me an answer right away. All he said was, "Let me think about it for a while." And that's as far as we got.

A number of years passed and still Kamiya gave no sign of his intentions. I doubt that he had simply shelved my suggestion. He was probably biding his time, waiting for the right moment for a merger. To be perfectly honest, things were running smoothly at both companies. I didn't press him about it because there was no reason forcing us to set a hard-and-fast date for the merger. Still, while it would have been a bit of an exaggeration to call the idea of the merger part of my "grand company plan," viewed over the long run, there was no doubt that bringing the two companies back together would be in both of our interests.

In December 1975, Kamiya resigned as chairman of Toyota Motor Sales due to poor health. Already quite advanced in age, his condition failed to improve, and in December 1980 he passed away without ever having given a clear indication of his true feelings about a merger. Plans for the merger began to take definitive form only after his death. Management at both companies favored the merger, so all that remained was the timing. Obviously, the sooner the merger took place the better. Thirty years had already gone by since the split. As time went on, fewer and fewer people remembered what the old Toyota had been like. Thirty years is about how long it takes for a full turnover in the workforce.

The merger would merely bring back together the two halves of a whole that had been unnaturally broken apart, but employees at TMS saw things very differently. The company they had entered was Toyota Motor Sales, a company that sold Toyota vehicles. All of a sudden, this was to be combined with Toyota Motor, a company that produced cars. It would be a mistake for us to proceed based solely on our own understanding of the situation. We had to act with caution. The first outward sign of the impending merger was the appointment of Shoichiro Toyoda as president of Toyota Motor Sales in June 1981. By then, events had already begun taking their natural course, so although I said nothing to Shoichiro of my intention in appointing him president of TMS, there was no need to. I'm quite certain that he understood what I had in mind.

I settled on a final plan for the merger in December 1981. I sought the views—or endorsement, if you will—of four people: Shoichiro, Seisi Kato, who was chairman of TMS, Masaya Hanai, then chairman of TMC, and Tojiro Okamoto, the senior member of Toyota's "council of elders."

The merger was announced on January 25, 1982. The mass-circulation weeklies immediately dashed off stories relating how the merger was "a new campaign by Toyota Motor to streamline operations" and how, after the merger, we were going to "farm surplus sales staff out to the dealers." Such reports made more than a few TMS people apprehensive about the future.

All the bad press we received before the merger actually turned out to be a blessing in disguise. If we had felt that we were doing something wrong, then we would've had a hard time explaining the real purpose of the merger to the employees, but because we believed in what we were doing, this wasn't so difficult. When you explain to them exactly why what the press has said is mistaken, the workers are sympathetic to you. I think that the great majority of the employees trusted the company.

We immediately began staff exchanges, starting with low-level employees and working on up to middle managers the second year. In September 1984, we even traded senior managing directors. Four years have passed since the merger. The company has now gotten back squarely on its feet and the merger seems well on the road to success.

THE DOYEN OF TOYOTA ELDERS

I'd like to say something about Tojiro Okamoto here. When Taizo Ishida died in 1979, Okamoto became the doyen of Toyota elders, lending the company his support and guidance.

Okamoto had originally been with Toyo Menka. In 1932, after Sakichi started up Toyoda Spinning & Weaving in Nagoya, Risaburo asked his older brother, Ichizo Kodama, the head of Toyo Menka, to send over someone with managerial potential, whereupon Kodama recommended Okamoto.

Kodama had just one reservation about Okamoto. "The only thing that's wrong with Okamoto is that he looks far too young," he said. "A man who looks that young doesn't have an imposing presence. But Okamoto has ability, and since Toyoda doesn't yet have any skillful head managers, his youthful appearance shouldn't be much of a handicap."

Okamoto and Ishida, who was a distant relative of Kodama's and already working at Toyoda Spinning & Weaving at the time, apparently became fierce rivals. Ishida was born in November 1888 while Okamoto was born in July 1889, so there was only eight months' difference between the two. But their personalities differed entirely. Ishida would rattle on, saying whatever he pleased, but Okamoto spoke very little. When they were in their prime, they didn't get on very well together.

But by the time I got to know them, both Okamoto and Ishida were already mature men of age and experience and had grown quite close. To be sure, while they were young, they must have viewed each other as rivals. Yet I suspect that, at the same time, each also had a great deal of respect for the other.

When Kiichiro began making cars, Ishida was against the idea, but Okamoto supported him. Toyota owes its existence today to the fact that Okamoto, who was in charge of company funds, backed Kiichiro's plans. This explains why Okamoto was appointed an auditor of Toyota Motor Company right from the start.

I met Kodama on only one or two occasions, but I have known Okamoto for a very long time. Okamoto really hit it off well with my father, Heikichi. When he wanted a drinking partner, my father would call over Okamoto and the two of them would make a round of the pubs. He would usually be the first to go under the table, so Okamoto always had to bring him home to Oshikiri.

When I told Okamoto of the upcoming merger in December 1981, he was delighted at the news. He died two years later, on December 19, 1983, at the age of ninety-four. He was drinking and having supper with his son when suddenly he fell silent. His son took a closer look and found him dead.

It was Okamoto who had brought Shotaro Kamiya over from GM-Japan. Here's how the two of them first met. Kamiya entered

Mitsui & Co. in 1918 and was assigned to the company's Seattle office. At the time, Okamoto was working at Toyo Menka's Seattle office. Okamoto was nine years Kamiya's senior, and since both had graduated from Nagoya Commercial High School, he looked carefully after Kamiya. Toyo Menka had spun off from Mitsui's raw cotton division, so there wasn't a very strong sense of rivalry between the two.

Kamiya was later transferred to Mitsui & Co.'s London office. After several years there, he resigned from Mitsui and went into business for himself in London. But his venture proved unsuccessful, so he folded up his operations and returned to Japan, where he joined GM-Japan.

Some years later, Toyoda Automatic Loom Works had, after repeated attempts, at last begun to make trucks, but selling these was a totally different matter. Although the company was able to attract a good number of technical people, Japan didn't yet have any experts on selling automobiles—or if it did, they were working either at GM-Japan or Ford-Japan. With Okamoto's help, Kiichiro got Kamiya to come over from GM-Japan. Kamiya had been working in GM's advertising department, not in sales. He later admitted that his starting salary at Toyota was only one-fifth of what he had been making at GM. Yet, the cut in pay did nothing to dampen his enthusiasm.

Toyota owes a great debt of gratitude to Okamoto. Not only was he able to scrape together the money the company needed to get started, he also brought Kamiya over to Toyota.

Okamoto had a deep sense of responsibility. Since it was he who had recruited Kamiya, he always watched over what Kamiya was doing and would often let me know what he thought. He remained concerned right up to his death over whether the merger was doing well or not.

DECISIONS THAT COUNT

Aside from Kiichiro, the person who may well have had the greatest influence on me was Taizo Ishida, with whom I worked closely for so long. But I've learned a great deal from many of the people I've come into contact with up until now. My association with Executive Vice President Akai at the end of the war was short, but he taught me to look at things from different perspectives. I can't think of any one individual outside the company as having had an especially telling influence on me, but each one of us is affected in some way by many people. Nor is it only superiors whom we learn from. I know, for instance, that I have been influenced over the years by many people working under me.

One of my most memorable decisions in the many years that I've been in management at Toyota is surely the construction of the Motomachi Plant. I didn't decide on this mammoth project alone, however. I had Ishida's approval.

Preparations at the Fremont Plant in our joint venture with General Motors (NUMMI) were completed early in 1985, and a ceremony marking the occasion was held on April 4. But as far as decisions on overseas matters go, we had a lot more trouble negotiating with Ford. I personally had had some contact with Ford since before the war, and in 1950 had even studied there for a short while and toured their plants. Of the Big Three, I felt the closest to Ford, although that was definitely not the only factor guiding my decisions.

In any decision, the people at the top are just flag-wavers. It won't do to wave your flag and have no one follow you. Waving that flag in a way that makes people fall in line behind you is what makes a decision a good one.

When the company decided to build the Koromo Plant (today's Honsha Plant) before the war, Kiichiro was determined to use a new production system in the plant. It's as they say: "A new wine for a new flask." He had a precise idea of the system that he wanted to set up, but it was all in his head. Unless he got everyone to close ranks and march in step behind him, he didn't have the slightest hope for success.

He took the trouble—and it wasn't easy—to find a way to bring the workers around to his view and have them follow him. The *kanban* system that we use today was something Kiichiro tried to get off the ground fifty years ago. That's how hard it is to get your employees to follow you. He burned himself out working on this.

Kiichiro never told me where he got the idea for Toyota's production system, but what this comes down to in the last analysis is a system free of waste. The important thing is that Kiichiro didn't stop to worry about whether or not he could achieve such an ideal system. He simply went ahead and tried to do what was generally thought to be impossible. I suppose that he had either the conviction or the confidence that he could accomplish what he was after. But what made the real difference is that he did more than just think about it: he went ahead and put his ideas into practice.

Of course, there are many types of decisions. Take the case of our merger in 1982. I knew that a merger would be best for both companies, but the biggest problem was when and how to carry it out. It was a question of timing.

A decision may involve nothing more than a choice between right and left. The results in either case may be completely different, but a choice has to be made one way or the other. When this happens, one may as well decide by rolling a pair of dice. I've been fortunate in that I've never come across such a situation.

Progress in computer technology has given us a wealth of data to help us distinguish right from left, but the final decision always will be up to a human being.

EPILOGUE: THE ROAD AHEAD

For more than thirty years now, Japan has been almost too free of turmoil. Such a long period of nearly unbroken tranquillity may be unusual in recent history. But there is no denying that this has been most fortunate for Toyota.

The trade friction between Japan and the U.S. following the second oil shock is probably as close as we have come to a crisis. In the auto industry, this friction did not arise from a gap in strength between Japanese and American automakers. The rapid growth in the export of Japanese cars to the U.S. in the 1970s was the result of nothing other than an unexpected advantage given to the Japanese automakers by the two oil shocks. While those oil shocks were a stroke of bad luck for U.S. automakers, they were at the same time a piece of good luck for the Japanese auto industry. It was only to be expected that if Japan did well in the American market, the U.S. would fight back.

The Japanese industry still has a long way to go before closing the gap in strength with U.S. automakers. Detroit's Big Three continue to wield enormous power in the world of the automobile. According to *Fortune* magazine, Toyota is the world's third largest automaker after GM and Ford, but the distance between Toyota and the two leaders remains large. Even Chrysler, which just a few years ago was on the verge of collapse, posted higher 1984 earnings than Toyota.

Trade friction always is going to be around wherever there's competition in business. Conflict of this sort will disappear only if one side accepts total defeat. But complete capitulation by Japan is out of the question, as is a total routing of our trade partners. Because Japan depends on trade for its very existence, to give this up would be to roll over and die. The mere fact that such conflict arises is proof that we are alive and well. As long as Japan's auto industry must export cars in order to earn money for Japan's oil—and therefore for the nation's survival—I believe that we have no choice but to resolve the trade conflict as best we can within these limits. While I don't feel the need for a continuation of the present voluntary export restraints, I do recognize the need for prudence.

I'd like to end this book with some brief comments on the future of Toyota and the auto industry.

The single largest attraction of the automobile, quite obviously, is that we can get in and drive off whenever we want to. As long as there's a road going there, the car will take us whenever we wish to go. At one time, horses and oxen were the chief modes of transportation, but today these have been fully replaced by cars.

Will the automobile someday be replaced by some other form of private transportation? Frankly, there doesn't seem to be any reason to think so at the moment. Even supposing that some device were discovered in the near future that offered such promise, this would take at least a decade or two to be developed into a form readily accessible and useful to the layman. So I suspect that the automobile is going to be around for a good while yet as an important tool serving people everywhere.

Even today, less than one-fourth of the current world population enjoys the benefits of the automobile. So not only does the auto industry still have a long life ahead of it, but there remains plenty of room for growth. I usually make about two trips abroad each year. Just recently, when I added up the number of countries I had visited in the past, I came up with 43. There are currently 159 member states in the United Nations, and Toyota exports to 140 countries around the world. Even I, the chairman of Toyota, have visited less than one-third of the countries to which we export. The potential world market for cars remains a large one indeed.

In Japan, the number of vehicles owned now exceeds forty-four million, but nearly fifty million people hold driver's licenses, so there is still plenty of room for more vehicles right here at home. Nor is this necessarily the upper limit for vehicles in Japan. The day of the multi-car family will someday arrive here too. In fact, many farming families already own their second or third vehicle. In addition, the automobile is a piece of machinery, which means that it has to be replaced every so often. Replacement demand within Japan alone is now over five million units a year. This represents an essentially permanent demand base.

So the future of the auto industry is very bright indeed. But since the industry is a vigorously competitive one, this is no guarantee that Toyota's future is also bright. What the future holds in store for Toyota depends entirely on the people who work there.

I have to admit that even I have been very impressed by our balance sheet since the merger of Toyota Motor and Toyota Motor Sales in 1982. But once an automaker begins losing money, it's like stepping into quicksand. On the other hand, the moment you think that you've hit a peak, the show's over. There's no need to decide that the company has stopped growing. The very least a company must do to go on developing is to channel back enough profit to sustain and stimulate further growth. That profit is essential to the future well-being of the company.

I have no demands to make of Shoichiro and the current management team at Toyota. It's up to them to decide where to take the company. I myself never followed a program laid out for me by Kiichiro. Nor do I see any need to point out the way ahead to those after me.

The only wish I do have is that Toyota reach 10 percent of the global market. This was a goal I set for the company when I was president. We reached the 9 percent mark in 1982, so it would seem that we shouldn't have too much trouble reaching the "global 10." But this has turned out to be far more difficult than we thought, because although Toyota continues to grow, if the world market grows even faster, then our share of the market soon comes tumbling back down again.

People often say to me: "You've led a fortunate life, haven't you." But there's no way of knowing whether one has really been fortunate or not in life. And we have even less of an idea about the lives of others. I believe that the moment I tell myself "I've had a full and satisfying life," that will be the end. That's why I refuse to think about the type of life I've had.

I'm already well into my seventies, but no matter how old I

get, I intend always to embrace the future. It's the same with a company as with people: turn back and it's all over. You've got to look the future in the eye and step straight ahead.

定価2,700円
in Japan